# MY LIFE AS I LIVED IT

## By Caroline Lee Cutro

Also by Caroline Lee Cutro
*Easy-Reading Poetry*

Copyright © 2014 Caroline Lee Cutro
All rights reserved.

ISBN: 1482668602
ISBN 13: 9781482668605

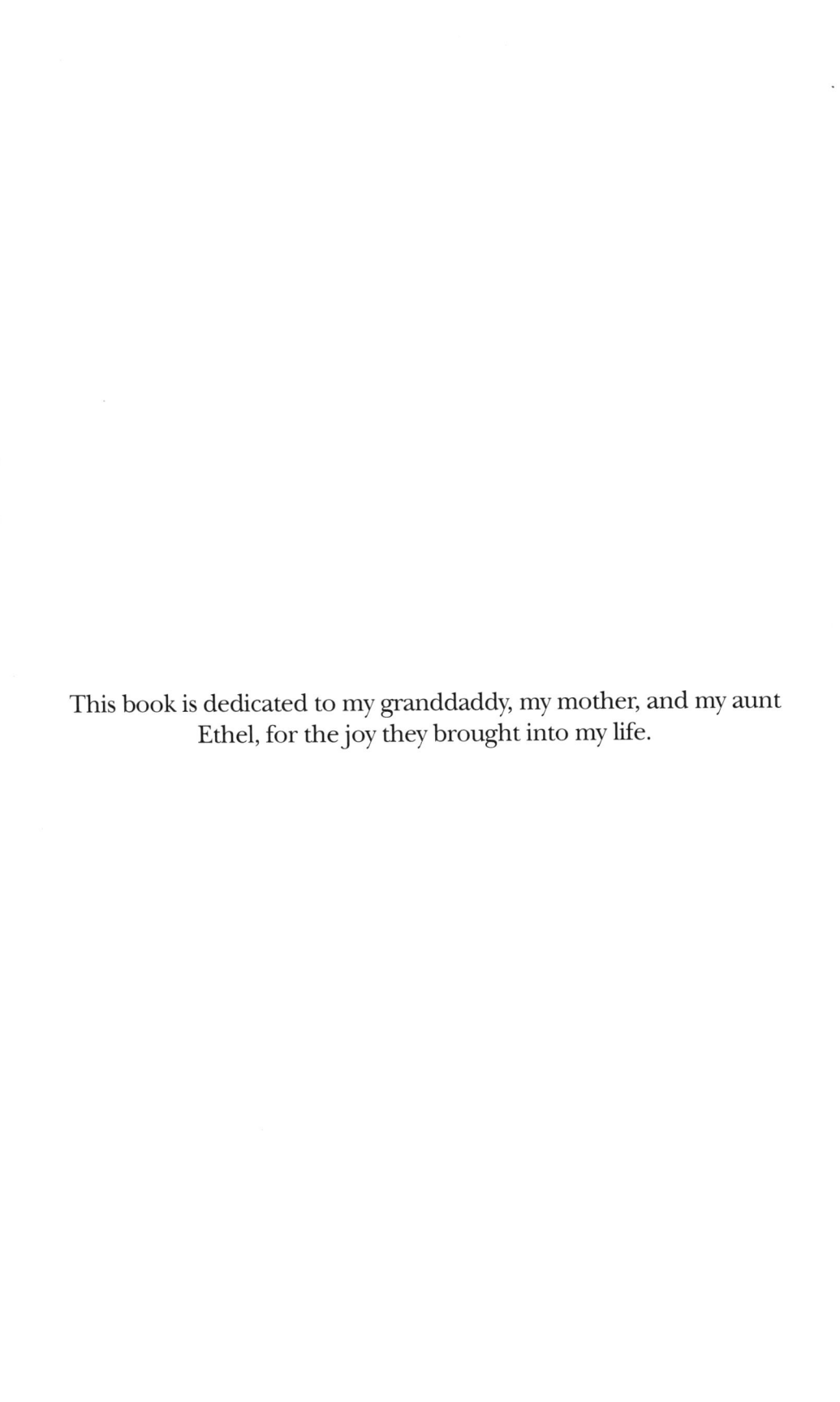

This book is dedicated to my granddaddy, my mother, and my aunt Ethel, for the joy they brought into my life.

# Foreword

I have been an editor and writer in the book publishing business for many years, so I have seen my share of books struggle to make their way into the world. When I read Caroline Cutro's manuscript, however, I knew right away that it would become the book you hold in your hand now due to what is commonly known as the sheer force of will. In Caroline's case, this is the same will that had sustained her throughout an often difficult childhood, her long marriage, raising a family, and starting countless successful businesses, from a hot dog stand to a sporting goods store to restaurants and retail shops to a thoroughbred horse farm, to name just a few of the Cutros' ventures. It's also the will that has kept her committed to seeking new experiences, learning, loving, and laughing for more than 70 years.

The stories that Caroline shares in *My Life As I Lived It* remind me of all of the little scraps and shreds of stories I love that my own mother has told me of her youth, and I savor especially the descriptions Caroline offers of a world and a way of life that for the most part don't exist anymore. Somehow reading her book also makes me feel like I haven't worked hard enough or had enough fun in my own life yet and I better get busy catching up on that!

Caroline has described her beloved family cottage in the Adirondack Mountains as her "cabin of memories," filled as it is with photos of generations of ancestors and furniture and other mementos that have stayed with her all these years. This book, *My Life As I Lived It*, is a treasure, too, a wonderful window on the past, from 1864 to the present, for generations to come.

Karen Watts
Karen Watts / Books

# Introduction

After my mother died, I was going through her photo album and saw all my great grandparents' pictures. I began to hang them on the wall in a little cabin my mom and I had in the Adirondack Mountains in Minerva, New York. We built the cabin 50 years ago and now it was time for a renovation. It was and is now my log cabin of memories. Everything tells a story. As I was hanging the pictures of my past generations, I longed to know what they thought. I felt I needed that so much. It left me with a feeling of emptiness, although emptiness isn't enough to describe my feelings. It made me feel unfulfilled and needing to know the thoughts and feelings my ancestors had during their lives. So I decided to write this book because I felt anxious when I realized that part of me was missing and I didn't want future generations of my family to feel that same anxiety. I just want them to know through my writing how I thought and felt and lived, not leaving anything for them to guess, wonder, or desire as I do.

I am leaving the cabin for my future generations so they can see how their ancestors looked and lived back in the 19$^{th}$ and 20$^{th}$ centuries. So I wrote *My Life As I Lived It* so they would know me—their mother, grandmother, and great grandmother—and their future generations to come could know me, too. I also wrote a book of poems of my innermost feelings about life. The book is called *Easy-Reading Poetry*. My husband, Nick, wrote a book called *For the Love of the Game*, about mostly funny things that happened during school, sports, and business.

I feel we have left no stone unturned that our future generations would wonder about. I always wrote poetry and short stories and said I could never write a book. I always tell my children, grandchildren, and great grandson "never say never" and I always try to prove it to them. I even surprise myself.

Maybe there will be another book because I would like to look up my roots going back through further generations of my German and Irish ancestry. I know that we all owned businesses, and now I can see it was all in our genes. We were all entrepreneurs, craftspeople, and natural performers.

The life I lived will keep my spirit alive for my future generations to come. They will know how I lived and struggled to survive, and my fears in life. This book is part sunshine and sadness, a gift to my descendants, so they can understand how I lived and see how the world changed from my birth in 1938 until now in my 70s.

### *If Only I Could Write*

*If only I could write*
*How wonderful it would be*
*To put my thoughts on paper*
*For generations to see.*

*There would be tender thoughts*
*And even some sad ones*
*Of what life was like for me*
*Living with all of you*
*In the 20th century.*

(From *Easy-Reading Poetry* by Caroline Lee Cutro)

# The beginning of my story

My German mother and Irish father met at my grandaddy's brother's bar and they fell deeply in love. My dad was a drinker even then, but my mother was so much in love that she thought her love for him would be enough to stop him from drinking. My mother married at the age of 20, while my dad was 26. Franklin Delano Roosevelt was president at the time.

I was born on November 14, 1938, in Margaret Hague Hospital in Jersey City, New Jersey. It was a snowy morning, which was unusual so early in November. I was named Caroline Ethel Lee—Caroline after my mother and her mother, and Ethel after my mother's sister. Two years later on December 28, 1940, my brother, William James Lee, Jr., was born. He was named after our father. my brother was called Billy and my Dad was called Bill. My mother was big Caroline and I was little Caroline. We lived in Bayonne, New Jersey, a small city located on a peninsula south of Jersey City that's surrounded by the New York Bay to the east, Newark Bay to the west, and Kill Van Kull to the south.

We had a hard time growing up because my father had the disease of alcoholism. He was violently abusive with my mother. I remember him beating her when she was pregnant with my brother. My brother was born with muscular dystrophy, which is a disease that is characterized by poor muscle control. He had to go to a special school called A Harry Moore in Jersey City.

Back when my brother and I were very young, my family lived on the second floor of a cold-water flat next to the train tracks on 11th Street in Bayonne. Some kind of peace came over me when the trains went by, probably because the sound of the trains would block out the sound of my parents fighting. The place was small, just two bedrooms and an eat-in kitchen. It had no hot water. Instead, we heated water on the stove and washed our clothes and took our baths in a deep sink in the kitchen. We bathed once a week, usually on Saturdays. I remember seeing my father bathing in that sink and he sure looked funny because he was so big. I guess my mother bathed in the sink, too. With no bathtub, we must have taken a lot of sponge baths. It was a two-family house. we lived on the second floor and the other family lived on the first floor. The other family in our house had two girls that I played with. We had a backyard where I remember playing house in the warm weather and playing in the snow in winter.

My grandmother's mother lived with us in a little room in the hall off the top of the steps, with just enough space for a cot-sized bed and a small stove to keep her warm. We called her Ma Ma Young. She was very old and frail and there were a lot of wrinkles on her face. Her daughter—my grandmother—Helen Young Lee and Helen's husband, Jimmy Lee, had a nice home in Bayonne and I thought Ma Ma Young should live with Helen instead of the dingy little room in our house. Besides she was afraid of my father when he was drunk. She would always close her door when my father came home.

Another memory I have of living on 11th Street was the time that my mother brought me inside from the cold with my snowsuit on and gave me some hot milk because it was very cold out. She didn't take the skim off of the top of the hot milk and she made me drink it with my winter clothes on, so I could go right back outside to play with the two girls that lived down stairs. I told her that I was going to throw up. I didn't want to, but I could not help myself.

I was gagging on the skim on the top of the milk. I also remember once when my father was coming up the stairs, bumping from wall to wall, and Ma Ma Young, so small and frail, ran to her bedroom. When he saw me, he put his finger to his lips for me to stay quiet and whispered, "I am only pretending to be drunk, but I'm not." There were no fights that night, so I guess he really was sober.

I called my grandparents, Helen and Jimmy, Grandma and Grandpa. She was small and he was tall. They looked like Mutt and Jeff but they always dressed nicely. My grandmother drove my grandfather to his job at Standard Oil Company in Bayonne so she could have the car. She was always dressed up like no one else I knew in town. I would hear people say, "Here she comes dressed like Nanny's pet billy goat." Grandpa was the quiet one. He used to take Grandma to the beauty parlor every week to have her hair and nails done. I know that makes him sound kind of mamby-pamby, but he was actually a tough guy. He served in the World War I and watched his buddy have his head blown off right next to him. Grandpa could not talk about the war even though he won a medal. When I was young, my mother once showed me Grandpa's medal from the service and she asked me if I wanted it and I said no. Maybe if she explained the importance of it I would have taken and treasured it.

My grandfather died when I was 13 and I remember they played "Taps" and fired a 21-gun salute at his funeral. At the time, I was very emotional. It seemed so sad that he had to experience all that killing that servicemen still do today.

When Dad took us to visit my Grandma's house—which I hated to do—she made my brother and I sit in one spot on the living room floor so we would not get her house dirty, as if we could. I would ask her to put the Victrola on so I could listen to "Jumbo the Elephant." Every time we visited it was the same thing. Once, though, my grandmother showed me her cedar chest. It was perfect. There was tissue paper between every item in the chest. She also had a wardrobe cabinet with a closet on one side and five drawers on the other. She was a perfectionist and a clean freak. I guess I took after her because my friends called me "Dustine" and always asked me if I caught the dust before it fell today. I always wanted Grandma's cedar chest because it made everything smell like cedar, so refreshing. Now I do have that chest in my little cottage in the Adirondack Mountains and it still smells like it did when I was young. It used to take us 12 hours to get to my cottage in the Adirondacks and now, with the Thruway and the Northway, it takes just 4 hours. When my great-great grandparents came to the mountains, they would take a train.

# 13<sup>th</sup> Street

When I was four we moved to another cold-water flat in the same neighborhood, just a couple of blocks away on 13<sup>th</sup> Street. The new house was a little bigger than the place on 11<sup>th</sup> Street, but still no hot water. I missed the steady sound of the train, but I could still hear the whistle. On one corner of our block was Hills Bar and on the other corner was a pharmacy. At the other end of the block were St. Mary's Church and a grocery store. In Bayonne, every block featured a bar on one corner and a church on the other. Bayonne is around 60 blocks from one end to the other and 3 miles wide. The streets had numbers not names, 1<sup>st</sup> Street to 60<sup>th</sup> Street, and avenues called A, B, C, D, and E. It was the easiest city to find your way around, uptown and downtown, east or west. Our house on 13<sup>th</sup> Street had a small porch that was about six feet wide. I remember watching a hurricane from that porch. Our street had become a river and with the water rushing by, I didn't dare step off that porch.

The Hill family lived above us. They had three girls older than I was. The older girl was the nicest and the prettiest. Her name was Patricia and she was always very sweet to me. I remember playing hide-and-go-seek with the neighborhood kids. One time an older boy called me "big eyes," maybe because I was watching him do something he shouldn't have been doing. I hated him calling me "big eyes" and for the longest time I kept looking in the mirror, wondering if I had big eyes. I never liked him after that.

The fighting was constant in our house. When I was about five, my mother and father got into a big argument. She said she just couldn't take it anymore. She said she was going down to the 16th Street Park and jump off the end of the dock into Newark Bay. I knew she would drown because she told me she didn't know how to swim. I ran upstairs to get help from the neighbors because I could not go all the way to 16th Street by myself and I wasn't allowed to cross the street. I begged for their help, but all they said was "Don't worry." I was so afraid to lose my mother because I didn't want my father to raise my brother and me. I was frantic but after what felt like such a long time, she eventually came home. I remember being so angry with her for causing me so much grief. My brother was really too young to understand.

I made my First Communion at St. Mary's Church in Bayonne on 13th Street, across from Main Street. I was six or seven. Grandma Helen and Grandpa Jimmy, my Irish father's parents, were there. He dressed in a suit, tie, overcoat, and a fedora. I remember her wearing a nice dress and coat and high-heeled shoes and a hat with a veil. I wondered how she walked in those heels because she was a little heavy and somewhat bow-legged.

She had a lot of beautiful hats that I loved. The ones with the veils over the face I liked the most. Sometimes when I went to dinner at her house alone she would let me try on her veiled hats. When Grandpa came home and we sat down to dinner I would watch him take his teeth out of his mouth to eat. It looked so funny, I thought, if only he could see himself! I tried to hide that I was watching him but I always wondered if he noticed I was staring. He didn't talk much. The only thing I remember him saying is, "Always be a good girl."

Other times when I visited by myself, my grandmother would cut an orange in half and load sugar on top. It was so good. "Now don't tell your mother," she'd say. "Oh, no, Grandma, I won't," I'd answer. Then she'd say, "Time for a nap." It was naptime not just for me but for her, too. She would fall asleep right away and I'd lay awake next to her the whole time watching and listening to her snore. She'd snore in and whistle out for the entire nap. It felt like her nap went on forever, but I lay there as still as could be, careful not to wake her.

When we first moved to 13$^{th}$ Street my mother sometimes left my brother and me alone in the house when we were two and four years old. She wanted to learn how to drive a car so she went with my father to practice. I was too young to realize this at the time, but she told me when I was older. I couldn't believe she could do such a thing, leaving us alone. She didn't think anything of it. I am sure in her mind we'd be just fine.

# Grammar school

When I was five and started grammar school two blocks away, I don't remember anyone walking me to and from school. My school was called Number 12 School on 12th Street. In the 2nd grade my mother gave me money so I could get cookies every day at school. The teacher kept a record of who paid three cents a week for cookies. There was a boy in school named Georgie Fadora who would always try to make me give him my cookie money by threatening to kiss me. I remember fighting with him about it, and sometimes I would give the money to him and sometimes not, but I know I never let him kiss me. After school I looked for the girls who lived upstairs to walk home with me, but that didn't happen much. I was always hiding from Georgie on my way home. I hated him so much that after all this time, I still remember his name. Eventually I didn't have to worry about Georgie Fadora anymore because we moved.

When I was eight, my mother began looking for an apartment house that had heat, hot water, and a bathtub. She found one on 8th Street across from the railroad station. It had three tiny bedrooms and the smallest bathroom in the world, but it did have a tub and hot water. It felt like such a luxury to take a bath, though we still only bathed once a week, on Saturday night for church on Sunday. Later in life I bathed every day.

This place we rented was full of cockroaches when we moved in. In the daytime we did not see them, but at night when we switched on the light, we could see them scatter all over. It was sickening to my little stomach. My mother soon got rid of them, though. We knew when we switched on the light at night and didn't see any that the roaches were gone.

There were four floors in the apartment building, with no elevator. I was sure glad to live on the first floor. My bedroom was very small, only big enough for a single bed and a dresser. There were many cracks in the wall that had been painted over, but I could still see them. At night, I would lay in bed after I said my prayers and look at the cracks in the walls and tried to make pictures out of them like I would do with the clouds. On Saturdays when I could sleep in, I would lie in bed and listen to fairy tales on the radio. But when I heard the kids playing in the alleyway and picking on my brother, I would get dressed as fast as I could and go outside to give them a piece of my mind and maybe a shove or two. I would let no one pick on my brother.

There were no refrigerators in those days. We had iceboxes with a compartment for ice that was delivered by the iceman once a week. The icebox had three little shelves for milk and cold cuts. I had to go to the store every day because it didn't hold much food. We did get milk delivered every day in quart bottles left by the door. The cream went to the top and on the days that it was freezing outside, the cream would freeze and pop the top off. My mother would give me around 30 cents a day to buy a loaf of white Wonder Bread for 19 cents and 10 cents worth of baloney. We only had about one slice of baloney each and if we had any lettuce or tomato from Grandaddy's farm, we would add that to our sandwiches. I still love baloney today, but I add more than just one slice to my sandwich today even though I know baloney isn't good for me.

When I was about eight and my brother was six my mother took us to the bar where she knew my father was drinking. It was a Friday and he had gotten his paycheck and went straight to the bar from work to pay his bar bill. The rent was due and my mother wanted to stop him from drinking the rest of his wages. Women and children were not allowed in bars back in the 1940s, so we stood outside and yelled, "Daddy, please come out" for a long time. We knew he was in there but he never came out. It was a hurtful time because everyone knew that my father was the drunk of the neighborhood. He always had black eyes from fighting, I guess. He would buy leeches to suck the blood out and make the black eye go away so he could go to work the next day. If he had a hangover, he'd make my mother call his work and lie about why he couldn't come in. He was a welder by trade.

My father was a drinker before my mother married him, but she was so deeply in love with him, she thought she could get him to stop drinking. She never stopped praying for him to stop drinking up until the day he died.

We had a deep sink in the kitchen for washing our clothes on a scrub board and we hung them outside on the clothesline to dry. I had a lot of my clothes given to me. I remember I had this ugly green winter coat that I hated. I don't know how long I had to wear it, but what choice did I have? Like everyone else back then, when my shoes wore through, I'd stuff newspaper in them to get more wear. In church, when the men knelt down I would see the bottom of the men's shoes were worn out just l like my dad's. Everyone had holes in their socks back then, so the woman of the house was always darning socks. I never knew where my clothes came from but I always kept them clean. One time my Grandma Helen bought me two dresses for my birthday. They looked like Christmas dresses and they were too fancy to wear to school but I did anyway. I looked like a princess but I felt silly.

It was often very cold in our apartment. They didn't turn on the heat in the apartment early enough in the morning for it to be warm when we got up to get ready for school. Instead, the heat would come on just as we were leaving for school. It was so cold I didn't want to get out of bed. On school days during the winter,

I would run through the parlor (what we call the living room today) and look out the window in hopes that it was snowing, so school would be canceled and I could get back under the covers in my bed.

I felt like I was the dumbest one at school because I didn't have anywhere to study due to all the fighting at my house. My mother didn't help me with school either because she was always busy sewing. The times that my father was not at home and I should have been doing homework, I was cooking and cleaning instead. My mother's mother died at the age of 32 and my mother had no role model to go by. She didn't know she should have been encouraging me in my schoolwork. My mother was wonderful at knitting and crocheting and it seemed to take up most of her time. I still have lots of her crochet work, including a beautiful bedspread she crocheted that took a year to make. One thing my mother taught me was how to clean house. Our house may have been chaotic because of all the fighting but it was always clean. She also taught me how to sew and I made my own clothes.

In 4th grade I remember being in the auditorium on stage with about 10 or 11 other kids and the teacher had me stand in the middle while we sang "Take Me Out to the Ballgame." I was proud to be in the middle. I would have thought they would put me at the end. I was so proud just to be chosen to perform, and when the teacher put me in the middle of the group, I felt so important.

My teachers always gave me high marks in writing. I knew back then I loved to write but never did it unless it was an assignment. I was a top speller and was always picked for the spelling bees. I was also often picked by my teachers to be a team leader, which was another thing that made me feel good. Otherwise, I felt like the dumbest kid in the class. What an awful feeling. Many years later, I went to a class reunion and one of the boys at my table heard me chatter away and told me that when we were in grammar school, he always thought I was deaf and dumb like another boy in our class was. Now I can't shut up!

One day I came to school and saw some girls in the coatroom peeking out and I asked them what they were doing. They said, "We are flirting with the boys, stupid." I didn't know what flirting was. I guess I was a late bloomer.

Mrs. O'Grady, the school nurse, checked us over once in a while. She was very pretty and so nice. She told me I had beautiful, perfect teeth and asked me why I painted my fingernails red. I told her it was because it didn't show the dirt under my fingernails. I immediately thought that was a stupid thing to say. Instead I should have asked her if she didn't like the red color or if she didn't want me to polish my nails because I would have done whatever she said.

All of the apartment buildings on our block shared the same backyard, which was full of what seemed like a hundred garbage cans. It always smelled bad back there. There were 8 apartment buildings with about 12 feet between them and sometimes we played there, but most of the time we played out front on the sidewalk. In those days, children mostly played together in front of their houses, on the front stoop or on the sidewalk. We did tricks with our yoyos, played hopscotch, kick-the-can, and hide-and-go-seek. We also rode bicycles and rollerskated with the kind of skates you strapped to the bottom of your shoe. I was always looking for something to do. I even figured out how to climb billboards, which I did a lot, usually by myself. Now looking back I know that was a very bad idea.

One hot summer day, a friend and I decided to walk up the four flights of stairs to the roof of our building to sunbathe. When that got boring one of us thought of jumping from one apartment roof to another. We gave it a lot of thought and were very tempted to do it, but decided not to jump because we just might not make it all the way across and it would be a four-story fall. We never went to the roof again in case next time we were tempted to jump we might think we could make it. That same friend taught me was how to spit. I use to bend my head over to spit, sometimes missing and making a bit of a mess. So my friend said, "Just take a deep breath and blow it out." I never missed after that. I still do that, outside, of course, when I am alone. Otherwise I do it ladylike, like my grandmother did, by spitting into a hanky.

I got a bike for Christmas one year and rode around and around our block because I was not allowed to cross the street, which had storefronts and a railroad station on the opposite side of the street. I would ride other kids on the handlebars, which now seems a little dangerous but it was fun and I was good at it. I was very good at sports and one of the best in grammar school at basketball. I was a good shot so they would always yell "Give it to Caroline, give it to Caroline." When I was in 6th grade I asked Santa for a basketball for Christmas. I was lucky to have gotten it because there was a basketball court at the park across the street from where we lived. The boys let me play with them because I was the only one with a basketball. They called me "Chicken" because they thought I was cute and they would say "Hi, Chicken," which I actually liked and I would wave and smile. My brother wasn't sports minded at all. He liked to play board games and especially chess, which he was good at.

When I was about 10 years old, my mother got a job at Western Electric in Kearny, New Jersey. We finally had some money coming in, but my mother was still very thrifty. She worked all the overtime she could get. I did all the shopping, cooking, and cleaning. Unfortunately, my brother was of no help. All he wanted to do was play chess with me. I loved my brother but did not like him for not helping me with all the household chores. It was our job to wash and dry the dishes and he'd say "Let's play chess for it." If he won, he'd always want to play another game, so

## My Life As I Lived It

he'd say, "Let's play two out of three." I usually ended up washing and drying the dishes myself.

I used to go to catechism class after school and I made my confirmation when I was 13. My Aunt Ethel made me a beautiful white dress and I wore the most beautiful white shoes in the world. They were my first shoes with a wedge and I felt like a princess. When I was in 7th grade, my father arranged for me to attend a Catholic school for a week during my school vacation. I loved to hear stories from the Bible and I had a great desire to be a nun. I dearly wanted to go to Catholic school but we couldn't afford it, so after that week, it was back to public school for me. My father attended a Catholic grammar school and was actually quite religious. When he was sober I would go to church with him, mostly when I was around 17. I watched how hard he prayed and he knew all the prayers. It is a terrible thing what being an alcoholic can do to a family.

One night my parents had a fight and my father kicked a crack in a panel on the door to our apartment. He never noticed the damage he caused and we never fixed it because we liked to be able to look through that thin crack and see who was coming down the long hall. We were only interested if it was our father. If it was him, we would scatter to our rooms and be very quiet, in hopes that there would not be a fight. We were glad that the crack was there.

When my mother, brother, and I left the house, we would put a match in the door before leaving. When we came home, if the match had dropped to the floor, we knew my father was home, so we'd be very careful not to make noise and head straight to our rooms with our stomachs churning. If the match was still there, we could go in knowing he was not home yet, smiling with great relief that we could do what we wanted.

My father had a sword, and once when we were riding on the Bayonne ferry, my mother threw the sword overboard. She had my brother and me look out for her so that no one was watching when she did it. She said she was afraid he might use it on her one day.

We never sat down together as a family to eat dinner except Sundays when we went to Grandaddy's farm. My father did not drink during those visits. There was no liquor at the farm so no one drank. My father did not always go with us to the farm. Sometimes he stayed home and slept it off. My mother cooked well for my father. He would get steak while us kids would get hamburgers and hotdogs unless we all had rabbit or chicken from my grandaddy's farm. One night, even though my mother was serving him a delicious steak, my father was so drunk and mean that he threw it across the room at her. I did not say anything but I wanted to go pick it up and eat it. Instead, my mom and dad got into another big fight and I was sent to my room by my mother so I would not get hurt trying to break up the fight, which I often tried to do.

Another night my father had my mother on the floor with a knife at her throat. I wanted to kill him before he killed her. I thought of getting our iron frying pan and hitting him over the head with it. If I killed him, though, I figured I'd wind up in jail, so I did the next best thing and called the cops again. This time I really didn't think they would make it on time, but thankfully they did. When we called the cops about my father and they would get to the house, my mother would never press charges. The next morning my parents would be passionately kissing each other like nothing had happened the night before. It made me sick. One night my father decided to put the gas stove jets on without lighting it. My mother smelled it, turned it off, and asked my father if he was trying to kill us so another big fight broke out. My father was mean every night, but when he was violently abusive, my mother would scream for me to call the cops. My little legs would be shaking as I waited out front for the cops to come because I feared that she would be killed before they got there.

In the 1940s and 1950s, the police were not strict about domestic abuse. My father did finally spend one year in jail for beating my mother. That was a very peaceful year. When I was growing up, sometimes I hated my father and remember thinking even then that he wasted his life. I always wished that I had a nice loving family like my cousin Dorothy had. I used to kneel next to my bed at night to say my prayers and ask God why I had a father like I did and my cousin had a wonderful father and family life. There was one period of about nine months that my father was sober and attended AA meetings. Those days are the best memories I have of my father from when I was young. I loved him and knew he could be kind but I felt sorry for his life and that our family life was so hellish.

# Going back generations

My great grandfather, Frederick Zimmer, and my great grandmother, Mary Adler Zimmer, owned a bar and restaurant called the Willows Rest in New Springville, Staten Island, New York. My great grandfather was an entertainer, with the unusual talent of being able to throw his voice. He was a ventriloquist without a puppet. People were drawn to his bar because it was so much fun there. I must have gotten the love of entertaining from my great grandfather, because I do love to entertain.

My great grandmother was a famous seamstress in Austria. I must have gotten my sewing ability from her. Sewing was my passion from age 12 until I was about 30 years old. By then I was so busy with three children that I stopped sewing. Before that, though, I made suits, coats, dresses, pants, blouses, prom dresses, all my maternity clothes and covers for furniture. I could sew anything.

Frederick and Mary Zimmer had four children: John Fred, Andrew, Rosie, and Madeline. My grandfather, John Fred, married Caroline Fett and they had two daughters, Caroline and Ethel, who were five and seven years old when their mother died. They were told that she died of a nervous breakdown but what really happened, we do not know. The Fett side of the family owned a flower shop called the Trolley Car in New Springville. I guess my love for flowers and plants came from the Fetts. It was passed on to me, my mom and Aunt Ethel, my two daughters, Carol Lee and Cindy, and to the next generation, my granddaughter Amy.

My mother's father was called Fred by some and Freddy by others but I called him Grandaddy. He was a farmer, a hunter, and a fisherman. My grandaddy had a couple of sisters, Rosie and Madeline. I was told that Rosie was beautiful. She was married but they say her husband was gay and all he did was sit in a chair all day. They took in a boarder and apparently the boarder fell deeply in love with Rosie and she with him. He did everything for her, waited on her all the time, and I was told her husband didn't care.

The other sister, Madeline, was married but got caught fooling around with another man and her husband, Earl, found out. He beat her so badly that she was in the hospital for quite some time, although she went back to living with him afterward. Later he had a stroke and after that, the only words he ever said were, "God damn." You could ask him "How are you?" and he would say, "God damn." Whatever question you had for him, the answer was always "God damn." We kids thought that was funny. I will never forget our parents telling us that Earl had been an enormous baby, weighing 17 pounds, 5 ounces at birth.

The next and last child of the Zimmer family, the youngest, was a brother named Andrew, whose nickname was Happy. I called him Uncle Happy. He was a fish and game warden in Staten Island, New York in the 1920s and was known as a staunch advocate of preservation of the environment on Staten Island. Happy inherited his parents' bar and restaurant down the hill from the farm and Grandaddy was left the farm. In those days, the Germans believed that the sons should get the inheritance while the girls would get nothing. Grandaddy's sisters didn't like getting nothing so, being resentful, they stole whatever they wanted from the house instead. During Prohibition the liquor for the bar was hidden on the farm by burying it under the ground and putting plants on top. It was also hidden under the haystacks and the cops never found it.

# My Life As I Lived It

Sometime in the early 1940s, when I was around seven, the bar burnt down to the ground. Everything was black ash. A priest was renting a room above the bar and when they were going through the ashes I remember them finding only one thing that hadn't been destroyed in the fire: the priest's prayer stole, which miraculously had remained perfectly white.

I was told that Grandaddy was a ladies' man. After his wife died, he moved to his parents' farm with his young daughters, my mom and my aunt Ethel. His mother and father wanted him home by 11 o'clock at night but he wouldn't come home at that time. So they told him he had to go live in one of the barns. He set up a little place for himself there, where my mom used to like to sit and talk with him. After his mom and dad died, Grandaddy moved into the farmhouse with his two girls. My mom always spent a lot of time with him. She loved to help him on the farm.

Grandaddy rode a motorcycle and drove his girls around on it. His daughters loved being with him so much and so did everyone else. He wanted to be independent. He had a farmhand drive him to different houses at night. He would go in the house for a while and the farmhand would wait in the car for him and then bring him back home. He was so handsome, I guess he *was* a ladies' man. He fell in love with the girls' schoolteacher and they were going to get married. My mother told me she did not like her teacher. My grandaddy got pneumonia and the teacher thought he was going to die and apparently she did not want to live without him, so she killed herself. That was sad because she left a son behind and my grandaddy did not die after all.

When Grandaddy took us grandkids for a ride in his car, he would always notice a pretty woman walking by and say to us kids, "Look at that hot tomato." We thought it was funny how he never missed spotting a pretty woman.

# Memories of Grandaddy's farm

Every Sunday as far back as I can remember, our family made the trip from Bayonne, New Jersey to Grandaddy's farm on Staten Island. That was in the 1940s, before the Verrazano-Narrows Bridge was built, back when Staten Island was all farm country.

We would take the Bayonne Ferry or the Bayonne Bridge to get there. The bridge was 25 cents a car then, but to save 15 cents we would take the ferry most of the time. The ferry no longer runs and today the Bayonne Bridge costs $12 to cross.

Once in a while I would go alone to the farm, either by walking over the bridge or by taking the ferry, and my Aunt Ethel would pick me up on the Staten Island side and drive me to the farm and I would stay the weekend. I do remember once walking across the bridge feeling afraid that someone would come along and throw me over the side and no one would ever find me. I never did that again.

When I went to the farm with my parents, we would often take a bus. There was only one bus that passed the farmhouse. We called it "the Red and Tan," which was the color of the bus. In the winter, if the bus came early and we missed it, we had to wait outside in the freezing cold until the next one came along an hour later.

Being a city girl, I loved going to the farm. When we got a car, we drove instead of taking the bus. Our old car would cough and sputter and threaten to give out in the middle of the road, but week after week it made the trip and never let us down. Our old "Tin Lizzy," as we called it, would make its way up the driveway to the heartwarming sight of the cozy old brown farmhouse. Everyone was glad to see us—my cousin Dorothy, my aunt Ethel (Dorothy's mother), my uncle, and Grandaddy. They all came out to meet us and they weren't the only ones. The ducks and chickens that flocked to the fence clucking and quacking, and the dogs barking, helped complete the happy welcoming. Yes, everyone was glad to see us.

Dorothy, who was a year younger than me, lived on the farm with her mother, father, and our grandfather. Grandaddy thought he was funny when he rubbed his rough beard on my tender face and tried to scare me when he popped out his false teeth as he greeted me with a big bear hug. He always laughed and despite all his teasing, we loved him very much. He liked when I helped him pick tomatoes and other vegetables from his garden. I hated to weed, but was always happy to help pick strawberries, eating as many as I could. Sun-warmed, fresh-picked strawberries were so juicy and sweet. The ripe tomatoes were, too.

There was a little airport about a half mile up the road from Grandaddy's farm that was used for a farmers' market every Saturday. We would all go to the market to help Grandaddy sell his vegetables. Dorothy and I were always happy to see our parents helping our grandaddy. They seemed to enjoy themselves and we loved to watch them sell. For some reason, it made me proud. Dot and I would walk around and see what the other farmers were selling their vegetables for and then we would report back to our parents. We felt we had an important job for seven- and eight-year-old children.

Grandaddy's farmhouse was really big, so at my suggestion, Dorothy and I would look for secret passageways, just like in the adventures in the movies back then. We would start on the second floor where there was one very small room that we just peeked at because there were too many old things in that room that didn't capture our interest and it was filled with dust and cobwebs. What did capture our interest was the door to the attic that had a table in front of it. We were warned never, ever to go in the attic. Of course, that just made us curious and want to go through that door even more.

So one day we moved the table, opened the door, and looked up the steep, dusty steps. It was very dark and spooky up there so we chickened out, closing the door and pushing the table back in place as fast as we could. Then we hurried back down to the first floor by sliding down the long, shiny mahogany banister. All we ever found were two very deep closets. One of these closets had a window in it so the light made it very bright and safe, but it did not look like a secret passageway, so we didn't bother with it. The other closet was very dark and we coached each other to go first. We peered in, held hands, and went in as far as we could go together and stood there for a moment. Then, getting a little scared, we backed out.

Next we went to the cellar where there was a kitchen stove. My great grandparents must have done some cooking down there at one time, probably for the farm hands and for their restaurant and bar, which was about 300 feet in front of the farmhouse. It was called the Willows Rest and it was a very popular bar year-round, even during the Prohibition era. Famous actors like Mary Pickford, Clara Bow, Douglas Fairbanks, Sr., Lillian Gish, Charlie Chaplin and other silent movie stars frequented the Willows Rest, where some would get drunk and sleep it off on the lawn outside the bar.

Next to the cellar kitchen there was a place where they dumped the coal for the enormous furnace used to heat the house or where you could get rid of a body, we used to say to scare ourselves. What a thought! Thinking such things was all part of the adventure we were having. Hanging from the rafters near the coal room were muskrat skins drying. Besides being a farmer, Grandaddy was also a hunter and a fisherman. Dorothy and I hoped we didn't eat what used to be inside those muskrat skins. After we'd spooked ourselves good, we quickly left the cellar and the adventure was over.

Now we did eat the ducks and chickens at the farm. We used to watch Grandaddy hold the chicken's legs and off came its head. Even after their heads were off, the chickens would run around and we thought they were chasing us. We ran, screaming, "Grandaddy, the chickens think we did it! They're not dead and they are chasing us because they think we did it!" When the chickens finally stopped moving, our mothers gathered them up and proceeded to dip them up and down in hot water and then pulled the feathers out. They saved the feathers for pillows and we knew we were going to have chicken that night for dinner.

Dot had a crippled chicken for a pet. I did not like that chicken and it did not like me. When Dot had to feed the chickens and collect the eggs, Dot would ask me to come into the chicken coop and help her. Knowing how much I disliked her crippled chicken, she would lock me in the coop with it and she would laugh as it jumped and pecked at me. It hurt! One time Dot even chased me into the house pushing that chicken at me. I ran in and up to the second floor and hid behind a door. She found me, though, and threw the ugly thing right at me. Then I ran from there down the stairs, and for protection, I squeezed behind my aunt Ethel who was lying on the couch and yelled, "Help me! Make her stop!"

Now, as for Dorothy's pet duck, who we called Dougie Duck, he was a great pet. We would take him for trips in the car, which he seemed to enjoy. Passing drivers would laugh when his head popped up, and we thought that was pretty funny. Like myself, Dougie Duck did not like the crippled chicken. I would have loved for them to kill that chicken and would have enjoyed every bite if we had him for dinner.

Dot and I were like sisters, which was nice because I didn't have a sister. Dot and I would tease my brother Billy awful, and we enjoyed every moment of it. One time our mothers took us shopping with them and at one store they bought underwear. While they were in another store, we sat in the car and held the underwear outside the window, hiding below the window so all the passing people saw only Billy and the underwear. He tried to beat us up but the more he tried, the more we laughed. If we had to sit in the car and wait for our moms, it was never boring. That day on the way back to the farm Billy gave our mothers an earful about how bad we were. I don't think they paid much attention to him, as they were happy shoppers.

I never wanted to miss a Sunday at the farm with all the activities. Sometimes all the family would go in the field and play baseball. At any time of the day Aunt Ethel might have company, so we never knew who was going to be there and it was always a surprise. Friends, neighbors, and family—everybody loved the farm and coming to visit because Aunt Ethel was a great hostess.

The farm next door to Grandaddy's farm had a riding horse named Pinto. The horse belonged to Victor, who was a couple of years older than Dorothy and me. Victor had a brother much older than us named Mike. The family was a real Italian family, fixing Mike up with a girl from Italy to marry, even though he had never met her. We were a little afraid of Mike. He was strong as bull and we thought of him as a little unstable. Victor taught us how to saddle a horse, ride, and trick ride. I even learned to jump on the horse from the back and rode bareback. Hey, I even felt like an Indian. He wanted us to exercise the horse as he was too busy and couldn't give the horse the time it needed. So almost every weekend we would ride. One Sunday Dorothy decided to practice jumping onto Pinto's back to surprise me when I got there, but the horse was grazing when she did it and Pinto kicked her in the chest badly. They thought maybe she broke her ribs, but mainly it just took her breath away, which scared her and her mother pretty good. So it was a few weeks before we rode again. We were too young to know not to go near the horse when he was eating and no one ever told us.

One Saturday Victor came over and asked if we wanted to go on a hayride. We got all excited so Dot and her mom, my mom, my brother, and I got ready with a flashlight and gas lantern just in case we didn't get back until night. We all hopped on the wagon and rode up the long hill to the golf course on Richmond Hill Road, singing songs and having fun. What a wonderful day. When we left the golf course and started down the hill to head for home, a linchpin broke causing the wagon to keep hitting the horse in the rear. Now it was up to Vic and Mike to figure what to do since it could not be fixed. We stayed on the wagon while Vic and Mike put the horse in the back of the wagon while they held the post, trying to stop the wagon from getting away from them on the steep hill. Cars kept passing us with shouts and laughter coming from their open windows. "You are doing it the wrong way! The horse is supposed to be in front!" they'd holler. Being teenagers we were so embarrassed, though we should have been scared because we were in a dangerous situation. Every step was an effort and Mike and Victor grunted all the way home. It was dark most of the way back and so it was good we brought a flashlight and gas lantern after all. Well, as you can imagine that was our last hayride with Victor and Mike.

No more hayrides, but we still went riding. Once Dorothy and I decided to ride to the farm on the other side of Grandaddy's farm. We had never gone there so this would be an adventure. I was in the saddle and Dorothy was behind me, holding onto my waist.

We did not gallop the horse, we just walked him in a leisurely way while taking a look at new surroundings. Right before we left the open fields to go in the woods, we saw something unusual and rode closer to get a better look. We got off the horse and climbed on top of a large cement slate, which was about four feet high and eight feet long. There was a name and a burial date carved on it, from the 18th or 19th century. It was spooky so we got back on Pinto and began to ride into the forest.

We rode for about an eighth of a mile into the woods when we saw an old shack and decided to get a closer look. That was a very bad decision. A dog started barking and I stopped the horse. Then an old man with a rifle appeared, yelling, "Get off my property!" He started shooting and running after us. The horse got scared and belted out of there as quickly as we could turn him around. Later Dorothy told me the old man had grabbed her leg and tried to pull her off. I didn't realize he had gotten so close. We galloped out of there as quickly as Pinto could take us and never looked behind us until we were almost home. We slowed Pinto down and tried to calm our racing hearts. Talking about what had happened, we decided the old man was a hermit and we vowed never to go back there again, which we didn't. I don't remember whether we told our parents and Grandaddy, but if we did, they saw we were okay and that was that. There was no further investigation and that was fine with us.

In the winter when it snowed, Victor would saddle Pinto and tie a sleigh behind the horse with some rope. He'd ride Pinto while Dot, Billy, and I rode in the sleigh behind. We loved it because he galloped the horse and our sleigh barely touched the snow for the entire ride. So when Vic got tired of riding and we still wanted to have more fun, he let me ride. I loved galloping that horse. I saw a lot of cowboy and Indian movies in those days and I felt like I was in the movies when I rode, just like John Wayne. To me, riding in the sleigh like that was a perfect day. We sure did laugh a lot.

The last time we rode Pinto, Dot and I took him through the woods to the golf course because there was plenty of galloping room there. It was nice walking the horse through the woods. It was peaceful listening to the birds singing and the brooks running while we looked for wild creatures we didn't really want to find. When we got to the dirt road that circled the golf course, I started to gallop, heading for the big hill that overlooked the small airport. I wanted to slow Pinto down but he would not and I could not stop him. He pushed himself harder and harder and we realized that if he didn't stop we were going over the other side of the hill to our deaths, also that if he stopped short, we would fly off of him to our deaths. He was straining so hard to get to the top of the very steep hill that he finally started to slow and stopped on his own. We did not enjoy standing there and looking over the overlook where our bodies might never have been found. We turned and went back to the dirt road. We walked for a while on the road to the golf course, but after a while I got tired of walking and took off again at a gallop. It felt like I was on a racehorse or the Indians where chasing us. Pinto was going so fast and it was so much fun until we were about to meet up with the highway. I tried to stop him, pulling on the reins as hard as I could, over and over again. I told Dorothy to jump off but she wouldn't. I told her I was going to push her off but she wouldn't let go of me. My whole body ached. On a last try, I took my feet out of the stirrups, wrapped them around Pinto's belly and when the horse's head came back I grabbed the bit piece in his mouth and pulled hard, knowing that our lives depended on it. It took 500 yards for him to stop but he did and I am here to tell the story and so is Dorothy.

It turns out that while we were having our brush with death, some man in a car was following us. We were walking the horse then, neither Pinto nor us wanting to gallop for the rest of the day. We just wanted to get the horse back home. We didn't know the man was there until we turned around. He stopped us and asked if we were professional riders. We told him we weren't and he said, "Wow,

# My Life As I Lived It

you would never know it! Can I take your picture?" We agreed, probably because we were still all shook up from the wild ride.

On the way back to the barn Dot and I wondered why that guy wanted to take our picture. Maybe he had one of those cameras that could see through our clothes, like the x-ray cameras at the hospital. We hoped we wouldn't see that man again. When we got back to the barn Victor gave us hell for bringing Pinto back so sweaty. If he only knew that the horse ran away with us and we nearly died. Dot and I vowed never to ride Pinto again and we didn't.

We had all kinds of fun at the farm, not all of it dangerous. Dot raised rabbits, for example. Snowball was our favorite. She was so white, fat, and fluffy. Dot sold most of the rabbits she raised to some man who she thought raised rabbits, too. Then one day she asked him what he did with the rabbits he bought from her and he told her he brought them to the hospital where they were used for research. Shocked, Dot told him not to come back and he never did.

One afternoon Grandaddy asked us if we wanted to sell some rabbits down by the highway and we thought that would be fun. So we got all set up and stayed out there until it was almost dark. Just as we were about to pack up to go home, a man stopped to buy a rabbit. We were excited to have a customer. He grabbed each of them by the ears and picked them up one at a time to feel their bodies. I told Dot I thought he meant to cook and eat the rabbit, so I asked him and he said, "Yes" and we told him, "No, our rabbits are for pets only." We were glad he told us the truth but our grandaddy was very upset with us for not selling the rabbit.

The worst part of having rabbits is when it is time to clean the cages. I think Dot always waited for me to come to the farm to help her clean the cages. It was a smelly, disgusting job. Sometimes a mother rabbit would die after giving birth so we would have to bring the babies in the house in a box and feed them with an eyedropper or a baby doll bottle until they were old enough to eat food. I was a good cousin and, like Dot, I loved rabbits so I always helped.

Grandaddy hunted for rabbits with a bow and arrow. He taught me how to use a 60-pound bow, which was tough. In high school, I dated a boy who taught me to use a gun in the cellar of a church that had a shooting range. Shooting came easily for me. I was so good at it they called me "Dead Eye." I never killed a living target, though, and never would.

Dot was like a sister to me when we were children and we are still like sisters today. I loved to stay over with her at the farm and have the roosters wake us up in the morning. It would make me feel so good. Even today I have a rooster alarm clock to remind me of those days.

Dot and her mom had a dog named Fluffy. She was a beautiful white dog, clean and well groomed. Grandaddy had a dachshund that was a nice dog, although I felt sorry for her because her coat was always full of fleas and ticks from running around in the woods with Grandaddy. He showed us how to burn the ticks off of his dog by lighting a match and touching the tick with the flame to make it fall off. It seemed like we did this all the time, though I would not do that today and I don't even know how I did it then. I would also let fishing worms crawl on my feet because it tickled and made me laugh. I am not that girl today.

Uncle Happy, my grandaddy's brother, had the property next to my grandaddy's farm. As a conservation officer and game warden, he started a fish and game club in the late 1920s in Staten Island, New York that is still in operation today. He offered youth classes covering a range of subjects from camping to conservation to hunting safety. The first year he registered more than a hundred 12- to 14-year-old boys and girls for his classes. Over the years, thousands of youngsters have participated in the programs he started. That same year, he started a Huckleberry Finn fishing contest, where kids dress up as Huck Finn and Becky Thatcher and win prizes for the best costumes. The contest took place at Willowbrook Park in Staten Island on the 4th of July, as it has every year since then. For the fishing contest, prizes are awarded for the first fish caught, for the smallest fish caught, and for the biggest fish caught. The night before the contest, Dot and I would get out our bamboo fishing poles and the water hose to wet the dirt so the worms would come to the surface. With flashlights in hand, we would fill our buckets with worms, so excited for the next day. Mostly we'd fish all day and not catch any fish but it was fun anyway. At the end of the day there was a party with all kinds of goodies to eat.

Uncle Happy was married to Anna and they had a son, named Andrew after his father. Andrew became a New York police officer and loved playing country songs at our farm gatherings. He divorced his first wife, who I don't remember being very nice. After he retired to Fort Lauderdale, Florida, he played music somewhere every night. He sang and so did his second wife. Andrew had two children with his first wife, a son and daughter named Mark and Gail. They grew up and Mark had a daughter with his wife, and Gail had a son who she raised by herself who turned out to be very successful.

One day my brother Billy was playing under a picnic table on Uncle Happy's property when he came running up to the back porch of the farmhouse. He was screaming and crying, with what seemed like hundreds of bees chasing him. I never thought to laugh at it then and I still don't think of it as being funny today. Our moms came out and laid him on a blanket. They had Dot and I get dirt and water to make mud that they slathered on him from head to toe and front and back. He had to lie like that for a long time. It was a good thing he was not allergic to bee stings or he would not have survived. He sure got lots of attention that day, poor thing.

There was another time when Billy was about three, we were at the beach with our moms and Billy disappeared. My mom ran up and down the beach yelling, "Billy! Billy! Billy!" She was frantic. I never saw my mom like that and I was so scared. Finally he came out from under the boardwalk, no bees chasing him this time. That was a day we would never forget. My mother was about 26 then and I remember her looking so beautiful running up and down the beach even though she was a wreck. My mom had a dark complexion while Aunt Ethel had a light complexion and light hair, the result of their German ancestry. Dot was dark like my mom and I was light like Aunt Ethel. Dot's mom was 92 when she died and I look more like her, except my eyes. When I look in the mirror, it looks like my mom's eyes are looking back at me. Dot and I were always very close to our mothers and we have been a very close family our whole lives.

My aunt Ethel died in 1992, and was buried in the historical cemetery at the Asbury Methodist Church in New Springville, Staten Island. Ichabod Benet Crane is also buried thereN he is the man on which Washington Irving's "The Legend of Sleepy Hollow" is based.

Every Christmas Eve we'd go to church with Aunt Ethel and Dot, then go home to the big farmhouse. When we got there, Dot and I would find presents under the Christmas tree. We could never figure out how they got there. While we were at church, we'd look around to see if someone left to put out our presents, but no one ever did. Our mothers never told us the secret of how all those presents got under the tree. Aunt Ethel was active in the Asbury Methodist Church her whole life, so when it came time to bury her, we knew she would feel at home there.

# My Life As I Lived It

It was always a big treat to go to the Staten Island Zoo, most of all to see Jocko the gorilla. He was there until he was very old. I even brought my kids to see Jocko when they were young. He was a real bad boy. He would poop and throw it at people. He was a big draw at the zoo because he would always put a show on for everyone. No one ever left the zoo without seeing Jocko.

Not far from the zoo was Glove Lake. You could ride horses there and rent a boat for rowing. When I was a teenager, some nice young man took me there on a date. I sat in the boat looking pretty in a dress I had made myself, pretending I was in a movie. I remember watching him struggle while he rowed the boat, poor guy. I just wish I could remember his name.

One Mother's Day weekend everyone was at the farm, where there were 200 feet of lilac bushes in bloom, with the most beautiful smelling, light purple flowers. Someone got the idea to cut lilacs for the house and then someone else thought why not have Dorothy and Caroline sell cut lilacs down by the road. The moms and dads got out there and started making 25- and 35-cent bunches and we got started. We got so excited every time someone stopped to buy flowers. Money was hard to come by in those days and 25 cents was a lot. We kept our parents busy all day cutting more and more flowers. If it were not Mother's Day we probably would not have sold any. For our last sale, a fine lady got out of a shiny black car and bought two 35-cent bunches. We ran up to the house to tell our parents about the rich lady who bought two 35-cent bunches. We went on about her beautiful car and how pretty and nice she was. Dot and I never knew how much money we made that day because we didn't get to keep it. We did it for the fun of it and that was what we got out of it. Everyone working together like that, we all had fun.

Aunt Ethel called me her "other daughter." She was a wonderful part of going to the farm for me. She was always happy, full of love, and lots of fun. When we were teenagers I had a ponytail and Dot had short hair. Aunt Ethel sewed each of us a red felt skirt with a white poodle on it. We wore our skirts all through the 1950s with our bobby socks and saddle shoes. That was the style and we enjoyed being in style.

Aunt Ethel would serve home-cooked meals with food that was grown on the farm and it was very delicious. There were always at least nine of us around the table at dinnertime. Sometimes Aunt Ethel would fib a little and try to tell us she made a pot roast, but I knew it was venison, which I did not eat. So instead I ate the farm-grown vegetables and Aunt Ethel's famous homemade rhubarb pie. We always enjoyed talking and sharing funny stories while we ate. There was a lot of family time back then, not like today when everyone is rushing off somewhere. After the meal we went to the "parlor," as the older folks called it. This room wasn't like a family room, which is used often. The parlor was only for special occasions. That's where the whole family gathered around the upright piano, sometimes three deep, with us little ones crushed to the front. Dorothy's grandmother, Ruby Main, who was called Nana, was a concert pianist. She'd sit on that bench and play that old piano so beautifully. She and her husband, Willy Main, were from Scotland, and I loved hearing the Scottish brogue, especially Willy's. I loved to listen to him talk, even though I couldn't understand what he was saying most of the time. I thought I'd love to have had an accent like that. After graduating from the University of Glasgow in Scotland, he went to work for the government and became a very famous marine architect/ship designer. His drawings of ships were amazing. One of his nieces had a framed piece of his over her fireplace that was three feet high and six feet long.

The evening was for singing songs of the times from the sheet music, songs like "I'm Looking Over a Four Leaf Clover" and "How Much is that Doggie in the Window?" Even when we'd been singing for hours, we never wanted it to end. We'd all say, "One more, one more!" This went on every Sunday through the 1950s. We were such a happy group singing together.

Later in life when I got married and had children, I loved singing lullabies and old songs to them. When I'd sing in the car my kids would fall asleep. My husband, Nick, said they fell asleep so they wouldn't have to hear my singing. When the kids were old enough they'd say, "Mom, please don't sing," and Nick would turn up the radio so he wouldn't have to hear me.

Years later, when my grandchildren were born, I would sing them lullabies and all of the "oldies" that I could remember. They would start looking at me the same way my children did. They would laugh or shake their heads. Somehow singing got into my blood, even though I know I can't carry a tune. When I'm alone, if the old tunes are playing, I just belt them out the way I used to around the piano years ago. I'm so glad I lived during the years when there was only radio. There was more time spent with family then.

To tell a little more about radio, one night when I was three years old I remember something terrible came over the radio and everyone in the kitchen at the farm was crying. I remember hearing them yell, "They bombed Pearl Harbor!" It was very upsetting hearing everyone screaming like that for hours. I was so scared and even though I was so young, I will never forget that horrible day for the rest of my life. Life was very difficult during the war. When the screeching sound of the sirens blew all over at night, we had to keep the lights out and the shades down for fear of an enemy attack.

I remember when the war ended just like I remember when it began. I was in Bayonne riding in a car and all of the sudden everyone was running in the streets hugging one another and yelling: "The war is over! The war is over!"

# High school years

In high school everybody liked me. They wrote "To the Sweetest Girl" in my yearbook and that is how I knew my friends thought that I was a sweet girl. They didn't think I was stupid, as they had in grammar school. Luckily I was able to do most of my homework in study hall because I could not do it at home. I had top grades, except history was hard for me. In high school I ran for student council in my freshman year. I had to get up on stage and give a speech. I was proud of myself for doing that and it built my self-confidence.

I used to ice skate with the boys in the winter a lot. We would do tricks and dance together. We also liked to ride sleds in Hudson County Park in Bayonne, which had a double hill that made you fly up in the air and hit the ground. What fun we would have. I got roller skates for Christmas one year and we'd roller skate at the Bayonne roller rink. I was pretty good at skating, but I don't know how I could have been good at as it was almost impossible because my shoe size was five and the skates my mother bought me were a seven. She bought them in a larger size assuming I would grow into them but I never did. So she stuffed the skates with cotton to make them fit but it wasn't very comfortable.

The next year I became a cheerleader. I was captain of the cheerleaders and I would make up my own cheers. If I may say so, I was very good at it. I think if you love something so much you give more than 100 percent. I marched in the football game parades with the high school band and cheerleaders playing the glockenspiel. Marching in the football parade in my cheerleading outfit really gave me a thrill. If you ask anyone who went to Bayonne

High School back then, they would say we were the luckiest kids to have gone to that school. We have had many reunions since graduation and we still see a lot of each other and keep in touch.

I didn't know at the time, but the man who would become my husband was a football player in my school. In fact, he was in the homeroom next to mine for two years and I thought he was a bad guy because one time he got caught bringing wine to school. The bottles broke in his locker and everyone had to stand in front of their lockers as the principal walked down the hall inspecting the lockers. I remember seeing the principal speaking to the guy who did it, a fellow who was two grades ahead of me. He had real frizzy hair and a dark complexion. He was definitely not my type. Lots of boys asked me out in school. I investigated them first before I said yes because I wanted to make sure they had good reputations. I had to write their names down in a book so I could remember them all.

My high school days were the best days of my life. I was voted prettiest girl in the senior class yearbook. I did not know that I was pretty until then because I was never told that by anyone. Now I always tell my own grandchildren how beautiful and handsome they are because I would have liked to have known that growing up. In my high school days we all wore dresses or skirts and sweaters or blouses and underneath—would you believe—a girdle so our backsides didn't wiggle. We wore stockings or bobby socks and saddle shoes or suede bucks. Girls never wore pants to school or church and in church we wore hats. It sure was a lot different then than it is today.

> **Back Then**
>
> Sometimes I think about how different things were when I was young, compared to the way they are now. For example, in the 1940s and 1950s:

Men tipped their fedora hats every time they passed a lady.

Women always wore stockings because bare legs were considered shameful. Crooked seams on your stockings were considered sexy, however.

Men shook hands every time they greeted each other, even their own sons. They never hugged or kissed each other because those kinds of emotions weren't shown. They never told each other they loved each other, but now they hug and say "Love you."

Minimum wage was 50 cents an hour. A new car cost $1,500 and we thought that was a fortune.

Gasoline cost 17 cents a gallon. When we went for gas, we never filled up our tanks. Most everyone said, "A dollar's worth, please" and that gas would last for a week. Every time we got gas—even just a dollar's worth—the attendant checked the oil and washed the windshields.

Cars had no signal lights, so we had to drive around with the windows open to signal to other drivers when we were turning. It wasn't until the late 1950s and early 1960s that cars had directional signals, power steering, or air conditioning.

Groceries were $10 a week and people complained all the time about the prices going up, just like they do today.

When someone died, flower arrangements would hang on the front door of the person's home for a week. At an Italian funeral, "criers" were often hired to attend the mass.

> Always dressed in black, they would wail and cry and scream relentlessly throughout the service even though they didn't even know the person. They even threw themselves on the floor just to stir up the emotions of the mourners.
>
> There were no deodorants, so everyone smelled the same. If someone smelled bad, though, it was awful.
>
> Many kids' homes were heated with kerosene, so they reeked of kerosene at school, which was terrible.
>
> Memorial Day used to be known as Decoration Day, which happens to be the day on which I had my first date with Nick. Decoration Day was originally a remembrance of Union soldiers who had fallen during the Civil War, but as the country healed after the war, soldiers who died on both sides of the conflict were honored.

Our house was always clean but I was embarrassed to bring anyone there except the neighborhood children I played with when I was younger. Being around 15 when I dated in the 1950s, I had to have my dates pick me up at my home, of course. I wanted to pretend I lived somewhere else but that did not stop me from dating. I had a lot of dates, sometimes two a day! We would go to the movies or play sports together. I loved ending the dates kissing. In those days we just kissed with our mouths closed. At least that is how my dates went. There were a lot of dates but there were only three guys that I dated for any length of time.

I always checked out a guy before I went out with him. I wanted to make sure he had good intentions. One day in school a girl named Janet said her cousin Nick wanted to go out with me. I said, "Let me see his picture." I looked at his picture and was not impressed at all. His name was Nick Cutro and he'd been a football star at our high school. He was playing football in college but was home for the weekend when he saw me cheerleading at a high school football game and fell in love with me right away. I wasn't planning to go out with him but he called me one Memorial Day and I didn't have anything to do, so I agreed to go to the movies with him. He came to pick me up wearing a suit, a white shirt and tie, shiny black shoes, an overcoat, and a fedora hat. With a big cigar in his mouth, he looked like the Mafia. I heard my mother say, "Now I know my daughter will go out with anyone." He was very nice to me that night, so I didn't mind being friends with him.

Nick's family would take me with them to his college games in Shippensburg, Pennsylvania, which was about four hours away. Nick had a fantastic football career at Shippensburg University. He was an All-Pennsylvania State Athletic Conference running and defensive back who helped the football team win the conference championship in 1957 and set a university record for the most yards per carry—an average of 13.2 yards—that still holds today. He was inducted into the Shippensburg University Athletics Hall of Fame in 1993.

I liked his family and they liked me, especially his mother. We really got along well. Nick's father had died a few months before Nick met me. His father was a fireman but also was an abusive drinker. His mother was a strong woman and kicked him out. She did a wonderful job raising seven children by herself. She was born on a ship in New York Harbor coming over from Sicily, Italy. Being born in New York Harbor made her a United States citizen.

# After high school

After high school my girlfriends entered me in a beauty contest in Bayonne. My mother didn't want me in the contest because she said that I would get a big head, but my girlfriends insisted. My mother came to the contest, though. It was the only thing she ever came to watch me do. She never came to watch me cheer even though I was proud to be a cheerleader and the captain of the squad.

I was worried that I had nothing to do for the talent competition. I liked performing on stage so I wrote and acted in my own comedy skit. In the middle of my skit, I saw my father come in and stagger down the aisle for a seat. I was so afraid that he was going to come on the stage. I did not know how I was going to keep the act up but somehow I did. The audience laughed out loud and loved my performance. In the end there was a three-way tie. I was first runner-up and got a beautiful trophy. The girl who won gave a better appearance since she was very tall and I was only 5'1", so I understood. I didn't care if I won, I just did it for fun. I was pleased, though, to win one of the three trophies. It sits in my house to this day.

Before the contest there was a parade in Bayonne and all the contestants rode in open convertibles, waving to the crowds. I was pleased with myself because I believed in myself and I made it happen. I could have said I can't do this or that but instead I just tried my best. I always tell my children and grandchildren never say you can't do it.

After graduation I worked in the secretarial pool at the Bayonne Navy Base where there were lots of sailors, soldiers, and Marines who were always flirting with me. What a nice feeling that would be to have right now! I did go out with some sailors and soldiers, as well as some higher-ranking officers, even if it was just for one or two dates. The higher-ranking officers would take me to the officers' club to show me off and all the girls in the office would be jealous. Working days were really fun for me. I was feeling really good in my life and the men I dated were all gentlemen.

There would be dances for all the servicemen where they had dance contests. I would always win, but I take no credit for it. I just had good partners and I could follow any great male dancer. If I got home late, my mother would beat the you-know-what out of me from one end of the hall to the other. Then she would listen to my explanation.

I wanted to go to college but my mother told me I would have to work my way. So at night after work I went to Grace Downs Airline School in New York City. Working all day and going to school at night was hard, but I enjoyed every moment of those days. At the end of the course, we had to do a skit for graduation. I guess I had the best ideas, because the girls made me the writer, director, and star of our skit. In the skit, I played an airline stewardess (of course) and my passengers were a drunk, a ballet dancer, a bratty kid, and a high-class lady, among a few others. It started with me introducing myself: "Hello, I'm Caroline Lee, 34-24-36, telephone number Federal 9-0000." Then the drunk comes up to try to measure me, and while I was trying to get him back to his seat, the ballet dancer was dancing all around and the bratty kid was screaming. It was bedlam. I can't remember the whole thing, but I do remember the teachers saying that of all the graduation skits they had seen, they enjoyed ours the most. That was nice to hear.

The girls and I spent a lot of time laughing, though I studied hard and graduated with high marks. The only problem was I wasn't old enough to fly. At that time you had to be 21 and I was only 18. I intended to become a stewardess when I turned 21, but got married instead.

I got to know New York City well during that time and I took my girlfriend Mary there to see Saturday afternoon plays. I had two close girlfriends in high school, Mary and Carol, and though we live in different states now, we are still close today. We were all cheerleaders in high school. We did everything together and double dated all the time. Mary and I discussed going to acting school. When I was in the Miss Bayonne contest, one of the judges was an actress and after the show she told me I was a natural. She suggested that I pursue acting, so Mary and I went to visit an acting school one night to New York. The address was in a hotel, which did not give us a good feeling but we went in anyway. It was interesting, but on the way home we had to take the subway. No one was around because it was late at night, which made us scared. So that was that. No acting school for us.

# Scared

There have been a few times in my life when I have gotten scared. Once my friend from airline school wanted me to show her Greenwich Village in Manhattan. She had never been there, so after class we went down to the Village and walked around. After a while I said we better get going because it was getting late and dark. We were standing in line for a bus and just as I was about to step onto the bus, a big black guy—over seven feet tall—bent over and whispered in my ear, "Meet me in Washington Square Park on Sunday." I felt my hair blowing from the breath of his voice. My feet could hardly make the steps of the bus. I had to get off the bus to take a subway and another bus home, afraid the whole time that he might follow me. I did not go there again.

Another time I was on a bus going home late at night from Jersey City and the bus driver picked some guy up who was acting weird. There were two other girls on the bus. He was looking at them and breathing heavy with his tongue hanging out. The girls got off the bus, leaving him and myself alone on the bus. He moved to the seat in front of me and turned around to stare at me, breathing heavy. I had to think fast if he was going to get off at where I had to get off because no one would be around to help if he tried to grab me. I remembered there was a candy store on 25$^{th}$ Street where my girlfriend lived, so I thought that I would get off there and run across the street into the store as fast as I could. I did that and sure enough, a few seconds later I saw the brake lights on the bus and he got off at the next block. Before he could see where I went, I ducked into the candy store, begging the owner not to close. There was a phone booth in the store, so I called my mother and sat in the booth until she came. She brought an off-duty police office we knew with her. What a fright I had.

I probably shouldn't write these stories because I am getting the same feeling over again. I will tell two more and be done with it. I came home one afternoon from a friend's, and when I stepped into our house, some guy came in right after me. I turned around to see him and yelled, "Mom!" When she saw the guy, she said, "What do you want?" He mumbled something about having wrong house but then he started up the stairs. Then my mother woke my father who was asleep on the couch and told him what was happening. My father ran up the four flights of stairs to the roof but the guy was gone. He must have gone down the stairs and out the front door as my mother was getting my father.

Another time I came home late at night and I was kneeling down next to my bed saying my prayers, as I always did before I went to sleep. Suddenly I heard scratching, which at first I thought was my dog Queenie. I said, "Queenie, what are you doing under my bed? Come out of there right now." I looked under the bed and she wasn't there. I still heard the scratching noise, though, and then I noticed that my window was open. I peeked out the window and screamed. There was a man on the ledge and his black leather jacket was scratching against the concrete wall. He jumped down and ran off when I screamed. We discovered later that he had turned a garbage can upside down and climbed on top of the can to get to the four-inch ledge outside my window. I suspected everyone in the neighborhood for months and kept looking for that leather jacket that I saw that night. I wish I had not screamed because we probably would have caught him.

# Minerva

Years later, quite a bit after the war had ended, my grandaddy would go hunting and fishing in the town of Minerva in the Adirondack Mountains of upstate New York. He would go during the winter months when there was no farming business. In 1945, he bought a one-room log cabin in Minerva that had an outhouse and no running water. He got water from the neighbors and used a long handled scoop to drink water from a pail. There was no electricity, so he used gas lanterns. It was spooky to watch them burn out. He had a woodshed full of wood and he burned it in the potbelly stove that stood in the middle of the cabin. Next to the potbelly stove was a table where we had our meals and played cards. Grandaddy's cabin wasn't much by today's standards, but I loved spending time there. When it rained on the old tin roof, I loved to lie on the bed and listen. It was so calming and enjoyable. When the thunder and lightning came, Grandaddy would tell me God was bowling in heaven.

The town is so small, there was just one hotel that was built in 1908 but burned down in 2003. There is also a general store that must be over 100 years old. I remember going there with Grandaddy when I was little, and seeing old man Jones sitting by his potbelly stove in the middle of the store, with all the penny candy in jars on the counter. When Granddaddy would go to Minerva during hunting season, he would go to the general store and meet up with all the other deer hunters to talk about the deer that got away. When he was in Minerva hunting, he'd send us penny postcards because he missed us and we missed him, too.

He often went to North Creek to Mrs. Smith's restaurant for turkey dinner and her great apple pie. He'd also play cards with her there for hours. She loved when he brought her vegetables from his farm in Staten Island. We continued to go to Mrs. Smith's restaurant for years after Grandaddy died. When we opened our restaurant in Lake George, Mrs. Smith would come by for dinner after a day at the Saratoga racetrack every August. She enjoyed our food as much as we enjoyed hers.

I remember him driving his car home from Minerva to the farm with two deer strapped across the front of the car. Everyone was happy to have venison to eat except for me. It made me sad, though, because my mother had taken me to the movies to see *Bambi* and I sobbed so much she threatened never to take me to the movies again. She said nothing would make me stop the loud crying and I remember it was even hard to catch my breath.

As the years went by, Dot's mom and dad bought a log cabin next to my grandaddy's and we all enjoyed going to Minerva on vacation together. Then later, when I was 18, my mother told me that Grandaddy had given her property next to his and she asked me if I wanted a cabin. She told me if I gave her my whole paycheck, we would have enough to have a cottage frame built. Then she and I could finish the inside and outside. I was happy to accept her offer.

After the frame was up, the cottage was a lot of work to finish, but my mother, then 38 years old, could do anything. I was the helper. I learned to do so much from her while we worked on our cottage. When it was finished, we had our cottage close to Aunt Ethel's and Grandaddy's, each about 50 feet from each other. We had our own little village.

In the summertime we would go swimming in Minerva Lake and fishing in the creeks. In the winter we would ski, snowmobile, and ice fish. Over the years, seven generations of my family went to Minerva, starting with my great grandparents. They boarded at a Minerva guesthouse so their grandchildren, Caroline and Ethel, would not get polio, a contagious disease that was common at that time.

Dot and I loved going to Minerva. We had lots of friends there, including four boys in the neighborhood around the same age as Dot and me. We loved going to a barn nearby and climbing the ladder to the hayloft. We would walk across the big beam then jump in the haystack. As soon as we fell we got up, laughing our heads off, then ran back to the ladder to do it again. In the daytime we would swim or waterski on Minerva Lake. We would also ride up and down the dirt road in an old Model T Ford with a rumble seat. My girlfriend, who was two years older than me, drove. She didn't have a license and the car had no license plate, but we were on a private dirt road. At night we played cards, went to the movies, or went bowling. Sometimes we went square dancing with our families.

Before we went in the house at night we would stop to look up at the sky because it was so dark the sky was covered with stars and we would look for the Big Dipper, the Little Dipper, the North Star, and the Milky Way. My mother knew a lot of stars and she would point them out to me. We often saw falling stars and wished on every one we saw. The best sight of all was the Northern Lights. It was like a light show that you could watch for hours. When we went out at night we would go with our mothers and their friends because we were too young to go out with the boys yet.

When I was about 16, I was down at Minerva Lake Beach with my cousin and I couldn't stop staring at the guy with this stupid Mohawk haircut. He was at the beach with his cousin, too. So the two cousins and the two cousins started dating. I dated Doug with the Mohawk and Dot dated Doug's cousin Bobby. Their last name was Foote. We are still in touch today and Dorothy sees Bobby even now because he takes care of our cottages. We double-dated all the time and went swimming almost every afternoon and dancing every Saturday night. Our families loved having Doug and Bobby around and invited them to Staten Island and Bayonne to visit. And, no, they did not sleep in our beds. It was the couch for them, of course.

Doug joined the Navy and one winter when he was on leave he came to Staten Island and surprised everybody. My uncle spotted him coming up the driveway and I ran to meet him, pushing my little brother out of the way. Later on in the house, we were going into the parlor and there was mistletoe hanging above the door. My cousin Dorothy walked up to kiss him but Doug said to me, "I don't know where you came from, but you got to me before Dorothy. I guess you didn't want anyone else kissing my lips." Everyone saw this and laughed hysterically. I will never forget it, because that night Doug asked me to marry him. I told him yes right away. I was so thrilled. We called his family on the phone to tell them the news. I talked to his parents, who liked me, and I said, "I hope you are as happy about this as we are."

The next day was Sunday and I met Nick going to church so I stopped to tell him that I was engaged. Nick was so nice, I felt bad about telling him that I was engaged and thought of the many things that I would miss about going with him. Nick asked, "Where's the ring?" I told him we just hadn't gotten it yet. The next day I went to work and told everybody that I was engaged. They also wondered were the ring was.

I went home that night and got a phone call from Doug. He said he talked to his parents and they wanted us to get married but I would have to change my religion. Apparently they had trouble with the fact that I was Catholic. He told me that I didn't have to be Baptist like his family, just not Catholic. I went back to work the next day and told them that I was no longer engaged. It was hard to do but I wasn't going to convert my religion for any guy. I didn't ask him to change his religion! I decided to see a priest and tell him what happened. I asked him if I could keep seeing Doug if I wasn't going to marry him. The priest said that he didn't want me to see Doug anymore. I think he thought that I would eventually be intimate with Doug if we continued to see each other. I wasn't going to be one of those girls that lost pounds over a guy, so I set myself up with a date every night of the week. Nick was one of them.

# Nick

I went to church every Monday night. Nick knew I went to church on Mondays and he asked to go with me, so we had a steady date every Monday and usually one other night a week, too. I used to ask God, "Why can't you give me feelings toward Nick like I had toward Doug?" Nick was good to me and I liked his family very much. He was going to college, he was a gentleman, and he was funny. One night I was supposed to have a date with Nick but I stood him up because I was having so much fun on an afternoon date with somebody else. I called Nick and told him I wouldn't be home for a date with him that night. At the end of the date with the other guy, we were parked in front of my house in his mother's Corvette or his father's Cadillac. He always gave me a choice of which car I wanted to go out in. We kissed, then got out of the car and walked toward the house. Nick was standing at the doorway with his hands on his hips. I don't know how long he had been standing there, but long enough to see the action in the car. I told the guy who was walking me to the door, "That's the guy I stood up to stay out with you." The guy responded, "Oh, is that your brother?" He was afraid of the way Nick was looking at him, so he turned around and headed back to his car before he got too close to Nick.

Nick wouldn't let me go in the house. He said, "Get in my car, I want to talk to you." We drove down to the water, to the Kill Van Kull, a tidal strait between Bayonne and Staten Island where all the big ships and freighters go by. The moon was coming up over the water. It was a romantic sight and I don't remember talking much. I do remember him kissing me for a long time. He used to kiss me for hours, but no more now that we are in our 70s. I sure miss that part of my life.

When Nick met me, it seemed to be love at first sight and he wanted to marry me even though I was going with other guys. He said that we could get married and I could live with him at college. He even took me to a married friend's house at college to show me how wonderful it was. I had to be chaperoned when I visited him at college because my mother would never let me go alone. I told my girlfriends what a nice guy he was and what fun we had, but that I would not marry him if he was the last guy on earth. He would come home on the weekends just to see me, a four-hour ride each way. He would write me letters all the time and phoned a lot, too. I was annoyed because it put me in a difficult spot. He was in love with me, but I was not in love with him. He was always telling me, "I love you" but I told him that I couldn't say that. He did not even want to go back to college. I had to talk him into it every time he visited. I would tell him to study hard and go to church every Sunday. He would write to me and tell me he was doing everything I told him to do. He said when he got out of college we would see more of each other and things would change. "Don't tell me you love me until you are ready to marry me," he said.

I was still dating other guys five nights a week but that left two nights for Nick, which included our standing Monday night date at church and one other night. I began to have more fun with Nick and little by little I was seeing less of other guys and soon Nick had the full week. My family got to like him and they used to invite him up to the mountains in Minerva. He helped around the cottage and got to like Minerva very much, even though he slept on the couch, as always. (I was a virgin when I got married.)

I spent time with his family and he spent time with mine. Nick's mother had a Scottish boyfriend named Jack Brown who had a strong brogue. She was always as excited as a teenager to show me his picture. It is funny how Nick and I double-dated with them, even once at a drive-in movie. Jack was always singing his Scottish songs and I loved to listen to him talk. They got married a year before we did and moved to Hollywood, Florida, where they had a beautiful home. They left the house in Bayonne for Nick when they moved to Florida. One night while we were at his house, he told me—as usual—how much he loved me and I thought hard for a minute before saying, "I love you" back. He said, "I guess you are ready to marry me now." I don't know if I even said anything after that, but I knew I was stuck.

Not long after that, we went out dancing with friends one night and afterward we went back to Nick's house. Long before, his father had left him a beautiful ring that I always admired when Nick showed it off to me. Nick was in the kitchen and I was in the dining room when he said, "Go look at my ring and see how it's sparkling." I said, "Not again," but I went to look anyway. What I found was not his father's ring, but a beautiful engagement ring for me. I told him that it was a lovely ring, but yelled at him at the same time. "Why are you giving me this at the end of the night? Why didn't you give me this at the beginning of the night so I could show it off to my friends?" I don't remember how he responded. I do remember that it wasn't the most romantic proposal but I did put on the ring.

So Nick was the only one I dated from then on. We set our wedding date for later that year. He was teaching and coaching high school football in Bayonne. He also played football with the guys. When he broke his ribs playing, I had to paint and fix up the whole inside of his house by myself. I was working at the time, too, so I asked a girlfriend of mine from Germany to help me paint the house. When I think of it now I should have told him to get his buddies to do it.

We got married during Christmas vacation while he was off from his job teaching school. The wedding was in Bayonne at St.

Andrews Church on 4th Street. We flew to Hollywood, Florida for our honeymoon and stayed at Nick's mother's house, while she and Jack came up north and stayed in the house in Bayonne. Her house in Florida was so cheerful, brand new with all new furniture. I loved it so much, I felt like a princess. While we were in Florida, we went shopping for a car with Nick's oldest sister, Milly, and her husband, Charlie. They lived not far away in Coral Springs, Florida. We didn't have a car at home, so we decided to buy a car in Florida and drive it home to New Jersey. One day we went out by ourselves and I saw a car I liked, a beautiful white Cadillac. I told the salesman that was the car I wanted to buy. He said it was his car but would sell it to me for $600. We knew we would have to spend all our money on the car and wouldn't have much left for a vacation, but I wanted that car. We really couldn't afford it, but when we took it for a test drive, we could see our reflection in the store windows as we passed and I would say, "Look at us! Look at us!" We looked so good that we bought that car.

Nick's sister and her husband entertained us by taking us to the Orange Bowl and to the spectacular Orange Bowl Parade. Another day we went to airboat races, which was very exciting. We also went to a comedy club and to see a barbershop quartet performance. I think Nick's sister and her husband loved me more than Nick and I loved them right away, too. They were really good to us and we had so much fun with them.

Hollywood was a beautiful area in 1959 as it was all being developed. Nick's mother's house was close to Collins Avenue in North Miami where all the beautiful hotels were. At that time North Miami was all lit up like Las Vegas. I wanted to go and ride up and down to look at the beautiful hotels every night. We did a lot of riding around the area. We drove to Key West to go swimming and have a nice lobster dinner on the water. I never had lobster before but Nick said I would like it and I certainly did. We drove all the way back to Hollywood after dinner because we couldn't afford to stay overnight. We were on a narrow road and got a flat tire and it was a good thing Nick had a flashlight because I was scared out of my mind.

On the way home from our honeymoon, we got a ticket for speeding in Caroline County, North Carolina. The police did not care that we just got married and they didn't care if they put us in jail, either. We had just finished having breakfast and were driving on a steep downhill slope when we heard the siren. The officer who pulled us over said to follow him and he took us straight to court where they said pay up or spend the night in jail. We had only enough money left for gas and tolls to get home but we had to pay $25 or go to jail. So we paid and had $10 left to make it home. We arrived at home with 28 cents in Nick's pocket. We moved into his mother's house in Bayonne and she went back to her house in Hollywood with her husband.

# Our children

My best girlfriends and I got married just months apart—one of us in November, one in December, and one in January. Carol and Mary got pregnant on their honeymoons. Three months after my honeymoon they were wondering why I was not pregnant yet. The day I found out that I was pregnant, I was riding the bus home after an appointment with the doctor and I was so happy that I was telling everyone on the bus that I was pregnant. Carol, Mary, and I each had our first children—all boys—born a month apart. Later, we had our girls a month apart and then each of us had our third child, also girls, and again born just a month apart. So our children were all the same ages, although Mary went on to have two more. Together we wheeled our baby carriages up and down Broadway in Bayonne, where we lived for a year or two after we had our first babies.

*First born—Nicky Cutro, Jr.*

I was 22 when Nicky was born. I was a baby myself but I felt so grown up. It was so long ago. It was for real when they placed him in my arms. We were not playing house. He was my little boy, not a toy. He was tiny, though, just five pounds and I called him my little monkey, because his face was wrinkled. Maybe that is why he has hair all over his body today. We named him Nicky after his father, of course. I remember just after we brought him home from the hospital, I leaned over him so carefully to bandage his circumcision but I didn't think it was nice of him to pee in my eye. One thing I didn't like was washing diapers, so I got diaper service. My dad was visiting once and he saw me drop the dirty diaper in the diaper pail. He told me I was supposed to rinse the poo out of the diaper first. I said, "Why do you think I have diaper service? What do you think I'm paying them for?" He proceeded to show me how to rinse the diapers in the toilet. I did it but hated it every time. I thought, if I had to do that I may as well give up the diaper service, buy diapers, and wash them myself. I would have loved having disposable diapers. They would have been a great convenience but they didn't sell them in my day.

I only let my father come around on the days that he was not drinking. It was nice having him around then when he was sober. He had more sober days after I got married. He wasn't working and had no money. I saved the poo diapers for when he came around, when I had him wash the poo out. He said it was just ground food and I needed to get used to it.

Nicky was a handful growing up. He never would stay in his crib. He would cry to be let out. If I didn't let him out he would throw up on the red shag rug in his bedroom. It took me a whole day just to clean up the crib and the rug. No more throwing up, though, after he learned to climb out of the crib. When he first started escaping from his crib, I would swat his bottom and put him back in the crib, but he would get right back out. One night when he was about 18 months old, I sat in the rocking chair in his room and when he got out of his crib, I swatted his bottom then put him back in the crib. A minute or so later, he got back out again, I swatted his bottom, and put him back in the crib. This went on for two hours and I knew we were going to have to try something else. Nicky's sister was due to be born and she needed the crib so we bought him a bedroom set, a beautiful solid maple set we still have today that looks like new.

Having a bed didn't change much, though, because he kept getting up after we put him to bed. So we decided to try locking

# My Life As I Lived It

him in his room. One night after we'd tucked Nicky into bed, Nick and I were sitting on the front porch saying how quiet he was. Then here comes little Nicky walking down the blacktop driveway we had poured that day. Thank God he was wearing his footed pajamas. We never figured out how he jumped out of the window of his bedroom because it was about 15 feet from the ground. We nearly died when we saw him. We couldn't believe it that he didn't even have a scratch on him. I think he really *was* a monkey.

We didn't have a dryer back then so I hung our laundry on the clothesline that ran from outside Nicky's bedroom window to a pole out in the yard. One day I was hanging clothes on the line when Nicky saw me in his room and decided to get back at me by locking me inside. I started yelling out the window, "Help! Help! Help!" I was so worried about his being alone in the house because I didn't know what he would do next. Finally a neighbor from the apartment next door heard my screams and called from her window, "What's the matter, Caroline?" Practically crying I said, "My son has locked me in his bedroom! Can you come over? Please hurry!" So she came right over and let me out of Nicky's bedroom.

Another time I was having some girlfriends over one night and I wanted to get Nicky all cleaned up and ready for bed. He was in his pajamas smelling like a sweet little baby and I put him in the living room to watch the TV for a few minutes while I cleaned the bathtub. After I was finished I went into the living room to find him half in and half out of the fish tank. I had to bathe him all over again but this time I didn't let him out of the bathroom until I was finished cleaning it. The girls came and the rest of the night went well, but I am sure he was up during the party because he never slept. He liked to sit under the table and feel the girls' legs in their nylon stockings. He liked the girls even back then. Whenever he saw the cheerleaders cheering for the football teams on TV, he would ask his dad to bring them home with him.

When Nicky was 11 years old, he wrote this poem:

**The Last Leaf on the Tree**

*I live in Rutherford in a very big tree. I am dressed in red, yellow, orange and purple. People always stop to look at me and my pretty colors. I noticed a lot of my friends are falling to the ground. Pretty soon we will all fall and be raked up by someone.*

*Then it happened. A very strong wind came and blew all the leaves from the tree, including my family. I was the last leaf on the tree, trying to stay alive.*

*There I was alone with no one to talk to so I just sat on the branch crying. Winter came and it was very cold. Then it started to snow. It covered the tree and me. I knew I would be safe.*

*November 2, 1971*
*Nicky Cutro*

My husband was coaching high school, semi-pro, and professional football when Nicky was little. Nicky always said he was born in a locker room. He followed Nick all over and, of course, he played football through high school. He went to college for a year and then he went into business with Nick and me, building The Boardwalk Restaurant in Lake George, New York, where we moved from Rutherford, New Jersey when Nicky was a freshman. He built the docks and much of the restaurant itself. He was an amazing worker.

After the restaurant got going, he took over the marina part of the business, renting boats and jet-skis, pumping gas, and renting dock space. He repaired boats and went on to be the best on the lake at repairing boat engines and hulls. He knew all about boats and got into offshore powerboat racing. For 16 years he raced boats while he was also working at the marina. He was World Champion in 1983 and 1986, National Champion in 1987, and the HFC Pro Series Champion in 1987. He set records that haven't been broken yet.

His boat was named *The Boardwalk* and we sponsored his racing for a few years. It got too expensive for us to continue, so he found other sponsors. One weekend Donald Trump sponsored him. Nick and I and the whole crew were comped for three days at Trump's Castle in Atlantic City. We probably spent a lot of our money in the casino but we had fun.

Today Nicky owns a big marina and marine store on Lake George. He works too much, often around the clock, but some people are like that. I guess he took after his parents, though he owes a lot to his mother for teaching him how to be so organized. Nicky is single and happy. He just can't seem to find a girl like his mom. We have a lot of laughs together. He is funny just like me. Well, his father is pretty funny, too.

*Second born—Carol Lee*

I guess chasing Nicky around caused me to give birth to my second child a month early. Nick's sister Lillian took Nicky to her house to stay there until I gave birth. Nick was teaching school and coaching football in St. Mary's in Rutherford and one day he asked me if I wanted to have lunch. So we went to a restaurant and I ordered lasagna. I started to eat then told Nick the meal was giving me a pain in my stomach that would come and then go away. This happened four or five times, so I told Nick to drop me off at my girlfriend's house because I had a feeling I should not be alone that afternoon. As soon as I got to my friend's house I was thrown against the wall in pain. She did not want me to stay and told Nick to take me to hospital. I said, "I'll be okay, I just have to get my girdle off." Back then we wore maternity girdles under our maternity clothes. Against my will Nick took me to the hospital, but I did not want to get out of the car when we got there. He made me, though, and the minute I went through the door, I was thrown against the wall in pain again. At that moment a wheelchair was put under me and they rushed me up to the delivery room. I was on the table and pushed four times and out came this tiny little angel. She was delivered before Nick even got back to school, which was just 10 minutes away.

She weighed only a little over four pounds so they kept her in the hospital for a week. I remember my father came to the hospital to see her and he just kept staring at her through the window for a long time. I thought that it must have brought back memories of when I was born. We named her Carol Lee as my name was Caroline Lee. That was as close as I could get to naming her after me without giving her my name. She was colicky and cried for three months straight while Nicky wouldn't sleep and tore around the house on his tricycle. It was about to drive me crazy. Those three months were miserable for me. I remember at one point in two days I got four hours sleep. I asked Nick to help me because I was so tired. He said he had to face a classroom full of kids the next day and he needed his sleep, too. That's how it was in my day. The men didn't help much with the babies. When I had Nicky, my husband dropped me off at the hospital and went to a local bar to celebrate me having a baby. When Carol Lee was being born, he headed back to school.

After the three months of colic was over, the great thing was that I would put Carol Lee to bed at 5 o'clock in the evening and she would sleep all night. I couldn't wait for her to wake up in the morning because she would hold her little arms out for me to pick her up and love her. As soon as I heard her I would jump out of bed with a big smile. I would go in and lift her out of bed just to hug her. It wasn't all fun and games, though. One morning she must have pooped in her diaper, because when I went in to get her out of her crib it was all over her face and body. That did not put a smile on my face that morning. When I fed her baby food, after her peaches or dessert, she would projectile vomit all over me. Once my father babysat Carol Lee and then when I came home he said he would never do it again. Apparently she projectile vomited on him, too.

The doctors thought Carol Lee had cancer when she was three years old. I had to wait two weeks get the test results and I was a wreck. She did not have cancer, but that was the longest two weeks of my life. I liked taking care of her after the colic and vomiting stopped. She was a sweet, loving baby and I used to call her my little angel. She was an angel, except in one way—once she started talking, she talked *loud*. I used to tell her don't talk so loud because angels don't talk so loud. She still talks loud today.

When she made her First Communion, Carol Lee's wish was to have her hair done the way I got my hair done once a week back then. Well, the hairdresser gave her a style that was so high and unbecoming on a seven-year-old. Everyone gave us funny looks because they thought I put a wig on her. After that we had a party for her. We always had a big party and roasted a pig for each of the kids' First Communions. All the kids liked to watch the pigs eyes fall out, as did some of the adults, too.

Carol Lee gave me no trouble when she was growing up. She was always well liked. Everyone has always told me how wonderful she is and how lucky I am to have her. Carol Lee had one boyfriend in high school, Patrick, who joined the Marines and disarmed land mines. When he was away on duty, we read in the newspaper that a Marine was killed disarming a land mine and everyone was a wreck thinking it was Peppy, which is what everyone called him. We didn't hear for a week that it was not Peppy who had been killed. When he came home on leave Carol Lee said she was going back with him to his base. My husband and I said no daughter of ours was going to live with anyone at 18 unless she was married. We had to let her go because she couldn't live without him. So they got married as soon as they got to Camp Lejeune. Later they renewed their marriage vows, this time at the Sacred Heart Church in Lake George. It was a big wedding with a reception at our restaurant. I took care of the decorating with everything was done in red and white. There were white tablecloths and red napkins with a red rose at every place setting. All the waitresses were dressed in white pants and red shirts. They were so happy to be at Carol Lee's wedding reception even if they had to work.

Now Carol Lee and Peppy have been married for many years and still act like they are on their honeymoon. I've never seen a couple so in love for so long.

*Third born—Cindy*

My last child was born two and half years later and we called her Cindy. The first two years of her life, I was the perfect mother and she was the perfect baby. She never cried and I just loved taking care of her every minute of every day. I dressed her up like a little doll, she was just so beautiful. I was thinking of having more children until she turned to the Terrible Twos. It was like night and day—what a change! From that day forward she always gave me a hard time. She looked just like me when I was her age and still does. Sometimes I look at pictures of her in my photo albums and think that it's me.

One time I was shopping at the grocery store with Cindy and we were standing at the meat counter with another lady. Cindy said loudly, "Look at that ugly lady's face." I couldn't get out of there fast enough. I never knew what she was going to say. She often embarrassed me in front of Nick's football players and they always laughed.

Another time I went shopping for a refrigerator at Sears with my mother and the three kids. My mother asked me for my undivided attention for just a minute when Cindy, who was about two years old at the time, said, "I have to go to the bathroom." Concentrating on helping my mother, I didn't notice my daughter taking care of her needs all by herself on the display toilet in the Sears showroom. When she was finished, she jumped off the toilet with her pants down running toward me calling, "Mommy! Mommy!" I hid behind the refrigerator while I made her brother and sister go get her. We left the store right away because the manager was giving us dirty looks.

When Cindy was about three I taught her how to ski on the small hill in our yard. I would carry her up the hill with my shins turning black and blue from her skis hitting them. When I took the kids skiing, Cindy was always the youngest one on the slopes. One time Nicky and Carol Lee got on the chairlift in front of me and Cindy got on with me. When it was time to get off, I helped Cindy get off first but I couldn't get off because she was in my way and wouldn't move. I was stuck on the chairlift but I couldn't see leaving my three small children at the top of the mountain so I jumped off from about five feet above the ground. No bones broken, thank God. All my kids have been skiing ever since and are excellent skiers.

Whatever I did or however I dressed, Cindy always copied me. Every year for her school picture, she wore clothes from my closet. When I took a group belly dancing class, she begged for private lessons. Cindy also took singing lessons but she hated her teacher because he seemed to have his mind on me more than on her. I told him not to talk to me while he was giving her lessons because my daughter didn't like it. He said, "I don't take orders from a nine-year-old." Then he said to me, "Why don't you let me teach *you* how to sing?" We never went back to that guy.

I belonged at the time to a little theater group. When I started, they didn't believe that I had never had acting lessons. I had them in tears at the end of my 10-minute performance because of the very sad, convincing ending. So after Cindy watched me perform many times, she decided she was going to put on a play for school. She was only seven, but she wanted to be the star, the producer, the director, and do wardrobe. That didn't last long because the other girls didn't like being bossed around.

She was 10 years old when we moved to Lake George, New York. We opened six businesses in one year, so of course she had to mimic us by getting into her own business. Nick used to go to a lot of auctions because he needed restaurant equipment. Cindy was in the 6th grade and loved to go to auctions with him. She saw how it worked and wanted to go into her own auction business. She wanted all my costume jewelry so she could sell it at school during lunch. She would say, "I am having an auction today. I have some great stuff. Step right up and look at this jewelry. You can spend your lunch money on a gift for your mother or someone special." I didn't want to give her stuff but I could not take her bothering me about it, so I gave in.

This went on for a while until Cindy's teacher called me to let me know that another mother had called the school because she was concerned when her child gave her a diamond ring. The teacher asked me if I knew what Cindy was doing and I said yes. The teacher asked if the diamond ring was real and I said no so the teacher said that Cindy was not allowed to sell things at school anymore. Apparently that was the end of a successful business, as Cindy told me later in life she was making $20 a day in the 6th grade!

Cindy was always looking to make money. She checked for change in the telephone booths and she went around to all the arcades in town, where she became known as the "Arcade Queen." By then we were in the restaurant business and she was charging people a dollar to park in my parking lot, which I didn't know until somebody told me.

When Cindy graduated from high school we gave her a big old Cadillac Eldorado, bronze with a white interior. We wanted her to be safe in a big car. Everybody called it a pimp mobile. She crashed it a lot and always said somebody banged into her. We bought her a junk car next, which she banged up just as much as the first one.

After high school she went to equestrian school. At the time, we had a farm and bred and raced Thoroughbred horses. I even delivered a filly and named her Caroline's Girl. We also had a Thoroughbred named "Here Comes Cindy." That horse made us money, winning about seven races. Over the years we had about 40 racehorses. Cindy worked a couple of years exercising horses at a few stables. I watched her exercise a Thoroughbred one time and she really looked like a jockey. She was going so fast I watched with my mouth open. I couldn't believe it, she looked so professional.

Later she moved to Florida and I let her live in my little house in Tamarac. She started working for a jewelry company. It didn't pay much money and it was a long drive so she decided to also work weekends at flea markets. She started making a majority of her money at the flea market so she ended up quitting her job at the jewelry company. There goes my stuff again, I thought. Two men who worked at the flea market saw what a good worker she was and they offered her a job selling their stuff, which included sunglasses, chamois cloths, rug cleaner, and whatever else. She was so good at it she decided she would open her own business. Before long, she even had people working her three booths for her, including one person who translated French for the Canadians visiting Florida.

At just 21, Cindy was working incredibly hard. I always felt sorry for how hard she worked, lugging around the tables, booking all the fairs, and selling her products. She never missed a fair. The biggest fair was at the Meadowlands/Giants Stadium in the Rutherford, New Jersey, and lasted seven days. She hated it, but she made so much money that she couldn't give it up. She bought a little motor home so she could sleep in it at night at the smaller fairs. She would set up on Friday and work straight through Sunday.

During this same time, Cindy opened a business in Lake George Village selling sunglasses and the like. She had that business for 16 years. Then she decided to live in Florida year-round and just have employees work her store in Lake George. She started an Internet business in Florida that sells health products around the world. She did very well and bought a building, hired some employees, and that is what she is still doing today. She no longer wanted or needed her store in Lake George, so being a nice sister and a very generous person, she gave the store to Carol Lee, who owns it now.

Cindy married Crockett Herd a couple of years after moving to Florida fulltime. He had his own business, was well established, and she liked the way he treated her like a princess. They have a lot in common and enjoy travelling together. Nick and I took an Alaskan cruise with them and Crockett's family. They take us to Las Vegas with them once a year and sometimes on other trips, too. Cindy is very generous. She takes after her mom and dad, too.

# Football and sporting goods

For the first 15 years of our marriage, Nick taught high school and coached football. Nick got so many of the boys from St. Mary's High School in Rutherford, New Jersey full football scholarships to college. I was very proud of what he was doing and happy for those boys. Every time Nick had a football game, I was there with my mother and our three children.

While he was teaching and coaching, Nick bought a sporting goods store in Rutherford. After the kids started school, I started working at the store as a bookkeeper, then later hired a bookkeeper so I could concentrate on growing the business. I started traveling to schools selling sports uniforms and gym uniforms for gym class. Then I taught someone to do my job in sales and went back to developing new business. For example, when we sent out the engraving jobs for our trophies, they were never ready on time for our customers' awards banquets. So I bought an engraving machine and did the engraving on trophies myself. I had similar trouble with delivery of the lettering work for our customers' football, basketball, and baseball uniforms, which never arrived on time for the start of the sports season. So I developed the uniform printing business myself in the cellar of our home in Rutherford. I taught my girlfriend how to engrave the trophies so I could work on the uniform printing. After my husband started working with the New York Jets, I did the printing for the jackets for a camp Joe Namath was running. We got to be friends with Joe. He often invited us to go out with him and I wanted to but Nick didn't want to get fired by the new Jets coach Weeb Ewbank for hanging around with Joe.

The last Super Bowl championship that the Jets won, the team was made up of most of the players from the semi-pro team that Nick was coaching at the time. He scouted for the Jets, too. He went on to be head coach of the Philadelphia Bell football team, which was in a new league. He was so busy at that time that he wanted me to run the sporting goods store and take care of the kids and the house while he coached the Philadelphia team. I told him if I ran the store that I would take it very seriously and when he had a football game he would want me to be there, but I knew I would not be able to go and that would break up our marriage. So we sold the store, though his coaching job with the Philadelphia Bells only lasted a year or two. They bought equipment from our sporting goods store, but didn't pay their bill and didn't pay Nick for coaching, not wanting to go bankrupt, I guess.

One year when Nick was coaching the Hartford Knights football team in Hartford, Connecticut, the team had 17 wins and no losses. Next game, we flew to Las Vegas to play the Las Vegas Casinos. Unbeknownst to me, Jimmy the Greek had written in his column that Hartford was bringing their "New England-type of witch" (that was me) with them to Las Vegas. They had the Casinos' witch and astrologer Sybil Leek there to offset my "powers."

In the morning at breakfast, all of the players were saying "Good morning, witch" or "Hi, witch" or "Where is your broom?" to me. I asked Nick why all the players were calling me witch because I thought they liked me. He told me that Jimmy the Greek had called me a witch for helping the Hartford football team have a 17-0 season. We were traveling with a lawyer, who asked me if I wanted to sue Jimmy the Greek for defamation of character. I immediately said no, thank you, because I liked being written about. Hey, it doesn't happen much! I figured I'd just enjoy it and go home and hang the column up on the wall in my house.

Around the same time, when Nick was working for the Hartford Knights, we had great tickets for a Don Rickles show at the Theater in the Round in New Haven, Connecticut. Our seats were close to the stage, and when Rickles started calling people up on to the stage, he picked Nick. There were a couple of other guys on the stage, but Nick was doing a good job backing-and-forthing with Rickles, so he sent the other guys back to their seats and did a skit with Nick. Not knowing that Nick was a football coach, he had him do a football skit and Nick made a few jokes of his own and the crowd went crazy for it, as did Don Rickles.

So then Don Rickles started talking to Nick in a fake Indian language, to which Nick replied in his own fake Indian language and the crowd fell apart again. Rickles and Nick had a very, very funny show together that night. After the show ended, Rickles announced to the audience that there were some celebrities in the audience, and he said a few names and then called on the Hartford Knights football coach to stand up. When Nick stood up, Rickles nearly died of embarrassment and apologized to the audience because he had no idea that Nick was the coach when he called him up on the stage.

A few years later, Nick was in Las Vegas with his brother-in-law Carmine and went to see a Don Rickles show. Rickles was on stage and shining a bright light into the audience. The light passed over Nick and Carmine and Rickles said, "Wait, turn that light back, I think I know that guy." When the light came back on Nick, Rickles said, "Nick, is that you?" Nick said yes, and Rickles proceeded to tell the story of the show in New Haven, which he had never forgotten. He invited Nick backstage, but Nick couldn't make it. I'm sure that Don Rickles was as disappointed as Nick was.

When Nick was working for the New York Jets, a lot of people wanted to meet him. At one time, a casting director asked to be introduced to him. They got to talking and he asked Nick if he would like to be in a movie called *The Godfather*. Nick said, "Sure, why not?" He was excited when he came home to tell me and I was excited, too. I said, "You know, Nick, if you don't make it in football maybe you'll make it in the movies."

The next weekend, *The Newark Star-Ledger* had a full-page article about me in a series they ran in the Sunday paper called "The Woman Behind the Man." When they first called me about an interview, I was confused because the women they usually wrote about belonged to different organizations. When I told her I wasn't really like those women, she said, "Good, then this will make a refreshing story." She warned me that she didn't know anything about football, and I told her not to worry, I would tell her all the questions she should ask me.

The interview went well and when the article ran, I was surprised to see it was a full page of the newspaper, with four photographs—one of me, another with my family, one of me arranging flowers, and another of me holding Nick's trophy. Every time I read one of those articles about other women, there were only three photographs, so I was pleased that there were four photos in my article. That very week, the casting director who had spoken to Nick called me and said he had seen my picture in the newspaper and asked me if I wanted to be in *The Godfather*. My kids were two, four, and six years old, and I had no idea how I would pull it off, but I told him, "Yes, that would be great." So I got my sister-in-law to babysit and I went to meet with the casting director, who took me over to meet Billy Friedken, a director working on another movie. I walked into his office and called him by his first name because we seemed to be about the same age. I felt stupid afterward for not calling him "Mr. Friedkin" but he hired me anyway. Not long after the meeting, Nick and I were called and asked to be in his movie,

*The French Connection.* So we showed up on his film set, where I was going to appear in a bar scene and Nick was going to be in a scene in a luncheonette. When I left the house early that morning, I surprised the milkman, as I was dressed up like a girl going to a nightclub.

The filming of my scene took four days. On the last day, I got to meet Gene Hackman and Roy Scheider. Roy Schieder would become famous for starring in *Jaws* a few years later. Roy signed my copy of the book, *The French Connection*, and said, "Where have you been all my life?" Gene Hackman was married at the time, with a boy and two girls, just like Nick and me. We had a nice chat and that was the best part of being in *The French Connection,* which won an Academy Award that year. Then we called our casting director about being in *The Godfather* and told him, "Don't call us, we'll call you. Our lives are too busy!"

# Our house in Rutherford, New Jersey

We were looking for houses in Rutherford close to our sporting goods store and St. Mary's Catholic School where the kids were attending school. One day our real estate agent took us to see a house that was once owned by the parents of William Carlos Williams, the famous poet and doctor. His younger brother, Edgar, was also born in the house. He was a renowned architect who designed the World War I monument in Rutherford, as well as the town's post office, library and several mansions that required 30 servants to run.

When we first saw the house, it had not been lived in for 14 years and the kids in the neighborhood said the house was haunted. Well, it looked it, with all of the overgrown landscaping and covered with trees. The huge house sat on two lots and had four floors. I remember walking up the front steps together, with my husband, mother, the children and me all holding hands. There was a porch that surrounded half the house and double doors that opened into the largest entry that I had ever seen. The living room was very large with a beautiful imported Italian marble fireplace and floor-to-ceiling French doors. As we walked slowly through the house, we huddled together every time we opened a door because we were afraid of what we might find. There was a butler's pantry for the servants, with one door for going in, one door for going out, and another that led to the kitchen, which had a fireplace. Off the kitchen and the dining room was the library, which was the best of all. The library had a cathedral ceiling, the first I had ever seen, as I don't think there were any in those days. There were six ceiling panels hand-painted with wreaths and flowers, no doubt by Edgar Williams.

On the second floor, the master bedroom could fit a whole bedroom set and a living room set, too. Adjoining the master bedroom was an enormous dressing room that was big enough to be another bedroom. There were four other very large bedrooms and two baths on the second floor. The hallway was grand, maybe six feet wide. The maid's quarters on the fourth floor had to be accessed by pulling down the stairs from the ceiling and climbing up. I wouldn't have wanted to be the maid in that tiny little room.

After we looked at the house, Nick and I talked about it and the kids and I told him we could never live there. My husband said that he was going to buy it anyway. Knowing that I was a good decorator, he knew I could make it beautiful. He was right. It *was* beautiful. We all couldn't wait to move in. I loved the feeling I got walking through that house in Rutherford after it was finished. I felt like royalty walking around that house.

It's funny that I started writing poetry in that house. Maybe it was the spirit of William Carlos Williams inspiring me. We lived there for five years. We had grape arbors in the yard that a little man from Italy took care of. We made our own wine at home by stomping on the grapes. We had three kinds of grapes and I made a variety of jams and jellies. I also used to can my grandfather's tomatoes and make tomato sauce. I was a canner like my mother, my aunt, and their grandmother. Now Carol Lee makes her own jellies and wine, too.

# Lake George

After 15 years, Nick retired from football and we decided to open four gift stores called the Bowl and Board, one each in Bayonne, Glens Falls, Lake Placid, and Lake George. The stores sold all wooden products, like butcher blocks, bowls, and wooden toys including train sets and more. When I found out how much it cost to hire someone to arrange the shop windows, I said I can do that, so I decorated the windows and inside the stores, too. We rented a house in Lake George one summer running the first Bowl and Board store there and I loved the area so much I didn't want to go back to Rutherford.

Lake George is a special place. It was discovered in 1646 by Father Isaac Jogues, a French Jesuit missionary who named it Lac du Saint-Sacrement. Over 100 years later, during the French and Indian War, General William Johnson led British colonial forces to occupy the area and renamed it Lake George, in honor of King George II back in England. The lake itself, which is known as the "Queen of American Lakes," is 32 miles long and 3 miles across at its widest point. There are 165 islands on this beautiful body of water, which is so clean that the town of Lake George uses it for drinking water.

Soon we started looking at houses in Lake George. A relative of mine who worked for the Lake George Steamboat Company told me about this beautiful home for sale on the lake. I asked her how much it was and she didn't know, so Nick and I went to see it. It was the most beautiful house I had seen in my life, especially where it was located right on the lake. It sat on a hill with a great view, a sandy beach, a boathouse and a large guesthouse. The place had seven bedrooms on four floors and a beautiful glassed-in lakefront porch where we couldn't help imagining spending all our time. We knew that we could not afford it, but we had the nerve to meet with the seller anyway. The owner was an older lady living alone in the big house, which is why she wanted to sell it. We gave her $10,000 down and she agreed to hold the mortgage for us. Still I told Nick that I didn't know how we were going to pay for it. He said, "Well, if we can't pay for it, at least we will know how it is to live good for a while." We still live in this house nearly 40 years later and hope to stay here until we die.

The business was doing well and we all loved it. While I was running the Bowl and Board, my girlfriend Beth and I took our children early in the morning before school to the YMCA to do gymnastics. While they were doing that we played racquetball, which we loved. Afterwards, Beth would take the kids to school while I showered, then went to the mall to open my Bowl and Board store. My husband played racquetball with me sometimes and he hated when I beat him. Sometimes he brought a friend and it was those two against me and even then I won sometimes. During one game Nick tried to distract me from making a shot by dropping his sweats and showing his bare ass. Well, he did distract me and I wound up falling on the floor and laughing my own ass off.

While we had the Bowl and Board stores and we were new up in Lake George, we joined a bowling league with Beth and her husband. Beth and I were always laughing and giggling and didn't take it seriously, but my husband was competitive. I wasn't good at bowling, but if I wanted to live with him, I'd better get good at it. So every time I got up to throw the ball, there was no smile on my face because I had to take it seriously, which was not as much fun as the laughing and giggling was. In the end, we won the couples league championship and got trophies, of course. Believe it or not, I got a trophy for the most improved bowler. On Thanksgiving, all the women bowled in a tournament with a turkey for the top prize. Guess who the winner was?

# The Boardwalk

A year after we bought our house, my husband came home and told me that he bought the property next to our house on the lake. There was nothing on it except a tool shed, but it was 100 feet of waterfront property. I asked him how we were going to pay for it and he said that we were going to sell hotdogs, hamburgers, and sausage, peppers, and onion sandwiches from the shed. I remember thinking that I would be selling hot dogs for the rest of my life. The shed was so small only one person could fit in the kitchen at a time. Our lawyer told us it was not a good investment, as no one had ever had a successful business in that location, which was on a dead-end street. Nick said to the lawyer, "Draw up the papers."

The first day we were open we made $28. Every year after we built on an addition to the property, which eventually became a famous restaurant that once took in $42,000 in a day, the most we ever made in a single day. Since it was on a dead-end street, I wondered how could I get customers to go there and I came up with the name The Boardwalk Restaurant and Marina, because everyone who goes on vacation wants to go to the boardwalk, right? We decided that when we had a sit-down restaurant we would start a Sunday brunch. I made all the desserts from scratch—apple pie, pumpkin pie, chocolate pie, pecan pie, lemon meringue, strawberry shortcake, cookies, and muffins. One time around Thanksgiving I made 17 pumpkins pies, all from one pumpkin and all in one day. We also made apple pies using apples from our apple tree.

I handled all the advertising for the restaurant, including brochures, newspaper ads, and radio and television commercials. I even had a billboard along Northway 87 and every time we passed it I was so proud. I'd say to Nick, "That's our place! Doesn't the billboard look great?" My mind was always on the advertising. I wrote and directed our television commercials. Among my favorites were the ones with preschoolers, such as the one I did with my three-year-old grandson, dressed as a chef, tall hat and all, standing on a stool in front of the stove, tossing potatoes into a pot that was as big as he was, while my four-year-old granddaughter, greeted the guests. The rest of the preschoolers I dressed as adults waiting to be served. The boys wore men's hats and mustaches and the "ladies" were dressed for dancing. Many people came to The Boardwalk because of that commercial.

I also wrote my own radio spots and did my own newspaper and magazine ads using my own photography. I learned to do everything myself because I wanted to save money, but also because I enjoyed it. The funny thing was that many of the people in the media business that I worked with at the time wanted to hire me. I worked really hard during those years but I learned so much. I always felt I could do anything anyone else could do and that's something I always tell my children, grandchildren, and great grandson.

Every year I made new menus with different designs. I designed new t-shirts and sweatshirts every year and sold them to my customers at The Boardwalk. I thought they were great advertising for the restaurant. The biggest seller was one designed with a pirate's face on the front. People loved that one so much that I had to keep getting more printed. Once my nephew, who was in the service, told me that he saw a guy in Texas wearing our pirate shirt. I also wrote seasonal riddles and rhymes that ran in the newspaper, inviting people to come to The Boardwalk. People would tell me that they would get the paper, read what I wrote, then read the Ann Landers column. What a compliment for something that was so fun and easy for me to do.

# My Life As I Lived It

I was the hostess at the restaurant and I always tried to make my customers feel special. We had so many repeat customers, and a lot of new customers came from word of mouth. We always had a waiting list for dinner and every Saturday there was a two-hour wait. We were written up in *Time* magazine, *The New York Times*, and in many local newspapers.

I designed the interior of the restaurant with bright red and black carpet, beautiful red hanging globe lamps, red tablecloths, and white napkins. The rest of the restaurant was decorated with a lot of marine decor. At night the red globes reflected outside on the water. It was a lovely sight. One year I had the idea to install underwater lighting along the dock so when customers would take a walk on the dock after dinner at night, they could see the fish and beautiful colors in the water.

For 30 years I grew my own plants at The Boardwalk. Everyone was astonished by the grape ivy plants that I had grown and nurtured for so many years. No one had seen grape ivy plants that were 17 years old. I had to get up early before the restaurant opened to take care of the watering every day. Since there were two floors, I had about a hundred green plants in the restaurant. One whole side of the restaurant was all sliding glass doors facing the lake just four feet away. There were also hundreds flowering plants in flowerboxes along the railing outside the second floor of the restaurant.

The employees wore white pants and red Boardwalk shirts for uniforms, so when they walked around on the street my restaurant was always being advertised. I sold thousands of Boardwalk shirts to customers, too.

The bar at The Boardwalk was a 4-inch thick, native pine slab that was 18 feet long and 36 inches wide. All along the bar there were engraved images of tall ships. Some people came just to see the bar because it was very unusual, truly one of a kind. We had an additional bar and dining area upstairs that could hold 200 people for dinner. At 11 o'clock at night the upstairs became a nightclub where we had famous bands and singers, stand-up comedy, and more. I especially enjoyed disco dancing and I wasn't shy about getting the dancing started.

At The Boardwalk, we had entertainment every night in the summer. Every Monday night we had "The Gong Show," which was so much fun, we just laughed our heads off. Nothing could have been funnier and nobody ever wanted to miss that night. The restaurant was just packed. Once we had these people from Tahiti who walked on glass and swallowed fire. They put on a real show. We had the big bands on weekends and it was hard to get in the place, even with a cover charge. Years later we turned it into a comedy club and believe it or not, I became a stand-up comedian, writing and performing my own material. I would go home after work at midnight and write new material until three in the morning. I had so much fun doing it, I just always loved to see people laughing and happy. Customers came back year after year to see me perform and my son, Nicky, was always bringing his friends to see me. He and I have a great sense of humor and we have always been proud of each other's accomplishments.

Owning The Boardwalk for 30 years, we had many celebrity customers, which was fun. I have a photo of Matt Dillon standing with me on the deck of the restaurant when he was just a teenager. Dick Van Patten, who was in *I Remember Mama* and "Eight is Enough," and his son, Vince, who was a tennis pro and sports announcer, were also customers. Vince ended up spending a few days with Nicky at our house on Lake George. I remember watching him in his bathing suit, with his great body, taking a cold morning plunge in the lake.

Robin Williams came for lunch once and said to the waiter, "I just want to keep a low profile." Ron Howard and his family came for

Sunday brunch and Billy Joel once sat quietly at the end of the bar having a couple of drinks. Jim Nabors sat on our deck and ordered a hotdog. Carol Lee was his waitress and had him sign the guest check. When Nicky heard Jim Nabors was there, he ran up to the deck and said to him, "Surprise, surprise, surprise," which was the line for which Jim Nabors was famous when he played Gomer Pyle. Everyone got a good laugh out of that.

In the month of August, when the Saratoga racetrack was open, we'd get tons of trainers, owners, and tourists on Tuesdays, when the track was closed. On days the track was open, people would spend the day at the track and come to The Boardwalk for dinner. The actress Maureen Stapleton did that all the time. We had lots of political people and TV personalities come through the doors of the restaurant. We had two Congressmen's daughters waitress for us one year. We had a lot of fun in those days, with wet T-shirt contests, bikini contests, and more.

We hired lots of bands and singers as entertainment, and one week we had the Ink Spots, who were famous in the 1950s. We had a lot of fun with them and they loved being at The Boardwalk. We had a houseboat at the time and we would take them out and show them the most beautiful lake in the world. They said they would never forget the great days at The Boardwalk.

Every Monday night in the winter, a bunch of guys got together to watch "Monday Night Football" at The Boardwalk, leaving their wives with nothing to do so I decided to form a women's group called "Women of the Lake." I would spend my week going through the newspapers to see who was in town and then I would call and invite them to tell us of their experiences. Once we got my lawyer to come to the group. It turns out he was also a magician. What a wild night that was. We were screaming because we thought he was going to cut off my girlfriend Pam's hand doing a magic trick. We were afraid for her to put her hand into the prop and it was taking a long time for him to accomplish the trick, so we were all screaming, "Don't do it!" We were so afraid for her but after a lot of screaming, at the end of the trick, her hand was still there.

All the girls couldn't wait for what I would come up with for us to do the next week. There were about 20 members of the group and they were always excited to come. We had a hypnotist and psychics come, someone different every week. We learned how to do palmistry, numerology, and tarot cards. I was good at psychometry. I would hold a personal item in my hand and tell the person something in their past that nobody else knew. I was so accurate that I actually gave it up because it scared me.

One year a bunch of us girls booked a trip to North Miami, Florida. We went fishing, dancing, touring, swimming and, of course, sunned ourselves. We planned cross-country ski trips and other outdoor trips. In my opinion, we had more fun than the guys watching football every week. We couldn't wait for the next Monday to come around.

Let me tell you about Halloween. We made a big thing of it down at The Boardwalk and people looked forward to it every year. Everyone had to be dressed up in a costume to get in. We gave away a $300 prize for the best costume. We had the biggest crowd and the costumes were fabulous. We did this year after year while my kids were in school and The Boardwalk was open year-round. My kids always won the costume contests at school because I dressed them up so well.

One Halloween, Nick and I were alone in the house. I told him that I was going to take a shower so he needed to answer the doorbell if it rang. I ran up to the fourth floor and turned the water on so he could hear it running down the pipes while I snuck downstairs without him seeing me. I had taken all my clothes off and put on a black raincoat, men's black shoes, a black hat, and dark glasses. I proceeded to go outside and ring the doorbell. Nick was peering through the window on the door and looked a bit hesitant and scared. When he opened the door I opened my coat and said, "Trick or treat!" He was embarrassed and said, "Oh, lady I think you have the wrong house." He didn't recognize me. When he finally realized who I was, he didn't think it was funny but I thought it was so funny, I fell on the kitchen floor laughing my head off.

The Boardwalk was our social life. We enjoyed booking weddings and birthdays because everyone had a good time, including us. We even had a special request from one customer who liked my husband Nick so much that she wanted her family and friends to celebrate her repose at The Boardwalk after her death. We did catering on the islands on Lake George and also in people's homes. When we were new at the business, we picked up customers with reservations by boat on a 34-foot Owens called *The Boardwalk*. People felt pretty damn special getting picked up and brought back to their motels and homes by boat. Eventually we bought a boat that we renovated and turned into a pirate ship that was 42 feet long and 14 feet wide called *The Buccaneer*. It could hold 52 people and it had two cannons on board that we would shoot toward Fort William Henry and they would shoot back in return. *The Buccaneer* was booked mostly by schools for their classes. We all dressed in pirate costumes and took them out on the lake to find the buried treasure chest. We gave the children pirate hats and we had a store that sold cap guns, swords, and many more pirate items. If the kids didn't have enough money to pay for the items they picked out, I gave it to them anyway. We also booked birthdays and weddings on *The Buccaneer*. On Sundays we took our favorite customers out on the boat for joyrides.

# The marina

Around our second year in business with The Boardwalk, we bought some old boats to start a boat rental business. Eventually we added newer boats and we were the first on the lake to have jet skis. The business expanded because of my advertising. I advertised the jet skis by riding them myself in front of the big boats and along the shore. I would dress up fully clothed with a hat and sometimes I would carry my dog along. Other times I would do some trick riding. I used to prank the folks watching me from the big tour boats and beaches by purposely falling off of the jet ski, then waving my hand for the jet ski to come back to me. The folks watching were surprised because they didn't know that the jet skis were designed to circle back when someone fell off.

When I was about 40. I raced on jet skis with my son, Nicky, who was about 20 and I won the race. I was surprised to win because he was a professional offshore powerboat racer who had set a lot of records. Once I even rode on the shoulders of one of my employees, which I had never seen done before. Nicky could trick ride standing on his head. I even got my mother at age 60 to ride on the jet ski. She sure thought she was hot. What a big smile she had, though. I was so happy that she was happy.

We rented out dock space to a dive boat, so I decided to take scuba diving lessons and talked my daughter Carol Lee into doing it with me. She wasn't the best scuba buddy. You are always supposed to stay with your buddy but she didn't, which made me worry for her even though she was not worried for me. Carol Lee and I got certified and when Nick and I bought a house on the water in the

Florida Keys when the kids were teenagers, we could dive right outside the house and see all the tropical fish. The scuba diving there was spectacular.

We took the kids to our house in the Keys when they had a vacation from school. We all loved fishing down there. We had our own boat with a galley, sleeping quarters, and a stand-up lavatory. That's the only kind of boat I like. We also had a small boat for catching stone crab and lobster. Everyone liked to go out and watch Nick pick up the crates and see how many lobsters and crab had been caught. It was always a surprise how many were there. Now Nick spends six months out of the year in the Keys and fishes twice a week, although I don't fish anymore. For years, I went out on the boat fishing with Nick every day. So I did plenty of fishing, crabbing, and lobstering in my day. Now he just goes out with a bunch of guys and we don't own a boat anymore, but my son Nicky, who owns a marina on Lake George, says we can use one of his boats any time.

# Still more businesses

After owning The Boardwalk for a few years, the property next door came up for sale. It was a corner property that faced the main street in the village. The property had been used as a gas station that serviced cars in two repair bays. We were one of the first to add a convenience store to a gas station. Every year we added more to the property. We had a bakery, we sold ice cream and sub sandwiches, we were a Trailways bus terminal, and operated a Western Union office. A year later we bought the property on the other side of the gas station, which had been the First National Bank of Lake George. We turned it into a lunch deli and kept that going for a couple of years, then rented that space to a real estate company. Later we built another building between the gas station and the old bank building. We used that new space for a raw clam bar that sold clams, shrimp, lobster, and other seafood. Nick and I bought a refrigerated truck and drove four hours to Portland, Maine and bought five thousand lobsters and sometimes clams and fish. We used some of the lobsters at The Boardwalk and sold the rest wholesale to other businesses in the area. After many trips to Maine we hired someone else to do the trucking because it was so exhausting.

We ran the clam bar for a year and then leased it out to someone who did not do well so we took the building back and leased it to our daughter Cindy for 16 years for her business selling sunglasses and other miscellaneous items. She did very well with that space. We had so many different businesses in Lake George over the years that most people in town knew us pretty well. Not well enough, apparently, as one day when I was 40 or so, someone stopped me and told me that there was a rumor going around town about me. Astonished, I asked, "What?" She said people were saying that I was a Playboy Bunny before I got into business in Lake George. I said, "Why, that's the nicest rumor I ever heard. Do me a favor and don't tell anyone that it isn't true."

One of the great things about Lake George is that it's a summer *and* winter resort. The Lake George Winter Carnival has been the highlight of the winter for more than 50 years, with tons of activities on the frozen lake taking place every weekend during the month of February. For at least 15 years Nick volunteered all of his time to the success of the carnival. The night before the carnival began, we would hold a coronation ball and crown a queen of the carnival. The next day began with the carnival parade, followed by the beginning of all the activities on the lake.

There were all kinds of races on the lake during the carnival, including a motorcycle race. Oh, did young Nicky want to be in that race. He begged and begged me until he wore me down and I said okay because I thought the race would be straight up the lake. When the starting gun went off, all of the racers took off but Nicky, who couldn't get his bike started. All of the professional riders were racing all around him but he was going nowhere. I was furious and screaming, and wanted to drag him off the ice and away from the race before he got killed, but Nick stopped me and made me wait in our van until the race was over. Nicky never raced on the ice again, but he does have a motorcycle.

There were snowmobile races on the ice and West Point parachute drops. The Coney Island Polar Bear Club, founded in 1903, would come up for a swim during the carnival and invite people on the shore to join them. They would go in the water near the docks, where the water was aerated to keep it from freezing over. One year my then-teenaged daughter Carol Lee went in with the Polar Bears but never volunteered again. There were fishing contests for adults and kids, toboggan rides for kids, ice skating, hot air balloon rides, fantastic ice sculpture contests, outhouse racing, and broomball hockey, among many other activities. My favorite was a racecar called "The Rocket," which went 225 miles per hour over 20 inches of ice and drew 10,000 people to the lake that year.

Once we took a ride on a ski plane that landed on the lake during the carnival one year and took Nick and I over the snow-capped Adirondack Mountains. The flight took my breath away and I will never forget it. The day ended with a torchlight parade of hundreds of snowmobilers, along with fireworks and a long night of dancing.

The Olympics took place at Lake Placid in 1932 and North Creek became a popular recreational skiing destination. For a while, there were chartered overnight trains for skiers that left from Grand Central Station in New York City late on Friday evenings and arrived early the next morning in North Creek. In the winter of 1936, it was estimated that 25,000 skiers visited the area slopes that year, which was a boon to the local economy. Residents made extra money by boarding the skiers for $3 a day, for a warm bed and three hot meals. Of course, this was at the discomfort of the resident family's children, who were bumped out of their beds and had to sleep in the cellar in order to accommodate the strangers.

In 1968, before we moved to Lake George, we would take our three kids skiing at Snow Bowl in North Creek. Our sporting goods store in New Jersey rented ski equipment, so for four or five years, we'd go up to Snow Bowl on the weekends and holidays and rent out skis from a little hut. Nick worked the hut while I skied with the kids, who quickly became excellent skiers. There was a wonderful lodge there, with the biggest fieldstone fireplace I've ever seen. It went from floor to ceiling and nearly wall-to-wall. I loved going there to warm up on the cozy couches in front of the fireplace. We would spend the night at our little cottage in Minerva. If we wanted to go night skiing, we would go to West Mountain, which was a half an hour from our house in Lake George. The whole mountain was lit up for night skiers and we used to go there often.

Years later, the state built the famous Gore Mountain ski resort in North Creek, and sadly the old lodge is gone. There are discussions now about joining Gore Mountain (Big Gore) with Little Gore (formerly known as Snow Bowl), and the Saratoga-North Creek Railroad is talking about reviving the popular snow trains of the 1930s.

The train station at North Creek has a little history behind it. In the fall of 1901, then-Vice President Theodore Roosevelt was on a hunting trip on Mount Marcy, not far from North Creek, when he received a telegram that President William McKinley had been assassinated at the World's Fair in Buffalo on the morning of September 14th. So Roosevelt boarded the train at North Creek to make his way to Buffalo, where he was sworn in as President of the United States.

As if the winter didn't offer enough activity and entertainment, the summer was loaded as well. At 6.1 million acres and bigger than the Great Smoky Mountains; Yellowstone, Yosemite, and Glacier Parks; and the Grand Canyon combined, Adirondack Park was like a gigantic playground. We enjoyed camping, swimming, boating, water skiing, jet skiing, kayaking, wave running, rafting, tubing, fishing, horseback riding, and mountain climbing. Nearby there's Fort William Henry, Magic Forest, and Great Escape, which is like Disneyland. There are 15 museums in the area, including the amazing Adirondack Museum at Blue Mountain Lake. There is also shopping, movies, dinner theaters, outlet stores, miniature golf, and arcades. You could visit the Adirondack Buffalo Company, with its herd of 40 or so American bison or even a House of Frankenstein. There's a wax museum, rollerskating, and hot air balloon rides. Gore Mountain's Northwoods Gondola Skyrides offer an amazing view of the Adirondacks, as does hiking to the top of Prospect Mountain, with its 100-mile panoramic views. There are great restaurants, hotels, and motels, and day trips to the exotic zoo, the Natural Stone Bridge, the Railroads on Parade in Pottersville, Whiteface Mountain, the North Creek Railroad, and the North Creek Tannery Pond Community Center, which features live theater and musical performances. Canada and Vermont are not far away, as are Fort Ticonderoga and Niagara Falls.

That's not all. Lake George has activities that include parasailing, skydiving, and boat tours. Our weekly rodeo at the Painted Pony is the longest running weekly rodeo in the United States. If the mood strikes for an adventure, you can rent a moped or mountain bike and take in the area. A whole family can enjoy a ride in a horse and buggy around town or two people can be picked up and brought anywhere by the Adirondack Pedal Cab Company. The trolley services and chartered fishing boats are enjoyable after a quiet morning walk visiting the stores of Lake George Village. In nearby Lake Placid, visitors can see the where the 1932 and 1980 Winter Olympics were held. There is also North Pole, New York, which is known as "The Home of Santa's Workshop," and Ausable Chasm, which is famous for its hiking trails and gorgeous scenery.

Back in Lake George, you can see reenactments of famous incidents of the French and Indian War at Fort William Henry during the summer. You can also catch free live music every night at the amphitheater in Shepard Park in the middle of the town. People come from all over every Thursday night to see the beautiful fireworks set off on the lake between Shepard Park and my house.

Lake George tries to have an eventful weekend, every weekend. From Memorial Day weekend in May through Columbus Day weekend in October, the town has something special planned for every week. Some of our annual event weekends include the Elvis Presley festival, the Adirondack Balloon Festival, the Lake George Jazz Weekend, and the Warrensburg Garage Sale, which is known as the world's largest garage sale. There's also Americade, which lasts a week and is one of the bigger events in Lake George. It's a huge motorcycle touring rally that brings about 50,000 motorcycles to town. Other big weekends include the Classic Car Show as well as the Antique Classic Boat Show, and there are several arts and crafts events in the park during the season.

# My mother

At a young age I took care of my mother, brother, and our home. I was afraid to get married and leave my mother. I just did not know how she would be able to get along without me. I gave a lot of thought about leaving her before I got married. My husband, Nick, was good to her, though, and they really liked each other. We spent a lot of time with her and called her a few times a day. She came to our house almost every night after work. I spent most of my time with her as I loved my mom very much and it made me feel good to make her happy. We took her away every weekend when Nick was involved with football for 15 years. I was fortunate to have a good husband that let me go on vacations with my mother. I wrote a letter to my mother to tell her how much I loved her and this is what I wrote:

August 2000
Mom, my Best Friend,

I probably never said it enough, but I love you. It seems like we are almost the same age, and times are getting difficult for both of us. I liked it better when we were younger. We used to laugh a lot. We had more things to laugh about.

Remember when our dog Queenie would yawn every time we did? We were lying on your bed. I'd yawn, then you, then we noticed Queenie yawn. We tried it again and again. She kept yawning and we kept laughing. We laughed so hard it was difficult to get out another yawn. I really don't remember another time we laughed so hard it hurt.

Another time we laughed was when we were in Minerva and Nicky was about five years old. He kept calling me from his bed, "Mom, Mom, Mom!" We ignored his calls figuring he just wanted to get out of bed. Finally we said, "What now?"

He said, "There's a leak in the roof," and there was. So late as it was and tired as we were, we had to move beds around, change bedding, and put buckets under the leaks. It's not so funny for us until we reminisce about it.

Remember when Billy (who wouldn't spend a dime) paid me 50 cents to swallow a raw egg? It was the hardest thing I ever had to do. But he was so cheap, I had to squeeze that 50-cent piece out of him. While I was trying to swallow that egg and gagging, the laughter continued. Billy stopped laughing when he had to give me the 50 cents.

Do you recall how happy you were when Carol Lee was born? You raced to the hospital and got stopped by a cop. I forgot how you talked him out of giving you a ticket. I remember you came right away when each of the kids were born. I would spend so much time telling you about the birth detail by detail and you would listen attentively. We were really close and had wonderful years together. I wish we weren't getting older. Things are so much harder to do now.

How could we forget vacations? They were great, just you and me riding mopeds around and deep-sea diving in Bermuda, and in Hawaii, flying from island to island and taking a submarine tour there. I took you to Pearl Harbor, where you touched the plaque with the names of all the soldiers who died there, and you cried like a baby, remembering back to the radio broadcasts at the time of the Japanese bombing of Pearl Harbor.

Another time we rented a motor home and traveled through the Blue Ridge Mountains to the Natural Bridge in Virginia and the Sequoyah Caverns in Tennessee. We watched them jump off mountains in kites. Some professional was going to take me up to try it, but you wouldn't let them. You said I might break an arm and I had to drive the motor home. At a campground in Tennessee, I locked the key inside the motor home. Remember what a panic I was in, knocking on other trailers, asking strange men to help us? Later when I thought about it, I was pretty nervous because one guy's key fit our lock. But at the time I was so relieved that I said, "I have this restaurant in Lake George, come park your motor home anytime, everything will be on me." The next day we saw the Chattanooga Choo Choo, then we took the long way to Florida down the coast. Or maybe that was another trip, we had so many.

Another time we drove with our friend, Anna Kohrman, to Florida and we took the long way on Route 1. There we were, three girls in a silver Caddy with "WOW" license plates, riding on Daytona Beach with the sunroof open. We used the CB the whole trip and had everyone talking to us. Your CB handle was "Hot Foot." You always did put the pedal to the metal. I can't remember my handle for sure. Was it "Honey Bear" or "Honey Bee?" Anyway, we were three generations—Anna at 75, you at 55, and me at 35—having the best time of our lives. Anna said it was the best vacation in her whole life. I said we have to do it again and she said nothing could top the last one. We went on the east and west coast of Florida. I know it was one of the better vacations I ever had, us three girls. I loved that Anna had known some of my ancestors and had known you and I since the days we both were born. She was so full of spirit, right up until the day she died at 99 years of age.

Of course, we can't forget all the wonderful places we went during those 15 years while Nick was coaching football. Almost every weekend we'd be somewhere else during football season. He wanted you to have a good time because you had it so hard with my dad.

I can't count the many times we went to Florida. We stayed in North Miami at the Hawaiian Isle. Remember how the ventriloquist picked on me all during the show?

At the Monaco Hotel, one day at the pool my kids each won a trophy in the swim contest for their age group. The announcer said, "Nicky Cutro, New York, Carol Lee Cutro, New York, Cindy Cutro, New York." Then we overheard a woman say, "How the hell many kids does that lady have?"

We also went to motels in Fort Lauderdale by the Sea. That was before I bought my home there. We had so many other good times. It makes me sad to think we can't bring them back. And I am sorry I subjected you to so much of my disco dancing. I know you loved to watch me dance, but the music was so loud. Still you followed me around. Thanks, Mom, for everything. Life could not have been as wonderful without you. If I ever did write about all our happy memories it would fill a book. If I get out my picture album, I'll never end this letter. The years in Minerva would be a book in itself.

I was remembering the times we went with your cousin Andrew and his wife Jenny to hear him sing country and western at redneck bars and we brought the kids along. We were really excited when he got a gig in a Miami Beach hotel. We thought he was headed for the big time.

I have been a lucky daughter to have a mother who enjoyed being with me as much as I appreciated being with you. We were truly best friends. And I'm saying that in the past tense, only because we are both getting older, and we don't have much of that get up and go like we used to. I want you to know I miss you very much. I wish the good times could last forever. You living four hours away, you can't drive up to Lake George every weekend like you used to, and I could never drive four hours now. I don't know how I ever drove so much on the trips we took. Maybe it was because you did most of the driving while I read to you. You are 82 and you still drive four hours, even though it's only once a year now.

I'm sure my three kids would not have had so many wonderful times if it weren't for your being in their lives. It really was so simple to make each other happy back then. Even in the generations to come, I don't know if anyone will ever be fortunate enough to share the closeness we did.

I love you, Mom. Thanks for being my best friend and for being such a big part of my life, as we shared each other's joys and sorrows. From as far back I remember, or as soon as I could write, I always ended my postcards and letters to you with "I love you with all my heart and soul" and I mean it today.

Love and kisses,
Caroline

My dear mother was 86 when she died. My brother died of pancreatic cancer in 2002 at the age of 63. Billy battled and beat alcoholism during his adult life. Later in life, he got married and had children, a girl and a boy. His daughter had a beautiful baby girl before he died.

I found out that I had breast cancer at the same time I learned my brother had three months to live. I did not tell my mother then about my illness because I did not want her to worry about both of her children. I had my operation as soon as possible so I could get to Bayonne Hospital before my brother died. When I got there, he didn't want to talk to anyone. He just wanted to die.

He told me he was sorry he could not talk and I said, "You don't have to talk. You know I always could do enough talking for both of us." He laughed, which made me feel good, and I think he did, too. I feel close to my brother every time I think of him. I made him laugh for the last time and remember the fun times we had in our childhood. Near the end, my mother and I went to be with him every day until he died on July 22, 2002.

# Travels

When the kids were old enough to stay by themselves Nick and I traveled. We started out with the holy places in Israel, Mexico, Canada, and more. The islands in the Caribbean were next. Then we travelled through Europe by train along the Italian Riviera, from Lake Como to Sicily, where Nick's family was from. We went to Austria and Germany, where my mother's side of the family was from and Ireland where my father's side of the family was from. We went to Switzerland, Greece, Belgium, Holland, and even behind the Iron Curtain where I was afraid and saw and heard a lot. We took cruises to Alaska and throughout the Caribbean. I could write a book about my cruises and trips, the good, the bad, and the life-threatening ones. When Nick watched the kids, I would travel with my mother and to tell you the truth I sometimes had a better time with my mother than Nick because my mother liked to try different things like scuba diving. She would do whatever I planned for us and never got tired.

When I go with Nick he has all the say-so. I wish my mother was still with me, I miss her so much. I feel if you make someone happy you become happier yourself. I loved making my mother happy and you knew you did because she would glow all the time and sometimes cry at the thrill of being somewhere. Mom, Nick, and I followed Nicky around the country when he was racing. The longest trip was from Lake George to California, going through the northern states to go out west and the southern states when we came back east. We took my mother with us and she had a wonderful time sitting in the front seat with her first-born grandson, Nicky, whom she adored. I spent a lot of time sleeping in the motor home that time. I just don't like long trips. Nick didn't like the long trip either and flew home.

# Florida

After retiring from the restaurant business Nick and I bought another home in Boca Raton, Florida. I had to buy this house because I could not do what I had done before. I had breast cancer and radiation and I was never myself after that. My husband expected me to be just like I used to be and doing all the things he did. I didn't like watching him have all his fun and I couldn't join him. I also had a knee replacement go bad and other problems. I couldn't stand myself so I wanted to have my own house to be by myself. So I bought the house in Boca Raton and he kept the one in the Florida Keys and would come to visit me two or three days a week. I didn't have to cook or clean for him, I just had to take care of myself. I just had to find something that would interest me and I would enjoy so I bought a computer and started writing short stories.

I bought my first orchid plant in Boca Raton and there have been many, many more. The same is true of my roses. I have taken many pictures of them and all my gardens and houses. Flowers bring such joy to my heart and Nick now shares my love of flowers. I have flower gardens at all my houses so I always have flowers in my house. Now my daughters and granddaughters have flower gardens, too. I know future generations will enjoy them as much as we have.

In Boca, I have a large orchid and rose garden that I couldn't have up North so I always have orchids and roses in my house there. I buy other plants to have around the outside of the house, too. It seems like I can't go to the grocery store without coming home with more flowers. I live on a golf course and I have floor-to-ceiling sliding glass doors so I can see my flowers all the time. I just love being surrounded by flowers. I can't do much by myself, so when Nick visits we go grocery shopping and he helps me with a lot of things. I can't go into stores unless they have motorized carts. Boca Raton is a beautiful town known for being called the "City of Trees." Flowers are everywhere. It is so beautiful to ride around and I want to stay there as long as I can take care of myself with a little help.

# The grandchildren

My grandchildren had to paint something for school and they told me they couldn't do it. I told them never say you can't do it. I told them Grandma can't paint either, but I am going to try everything—watercolors, oils, acrylics, charcoals, pastels, and pen and ink. I liked to be involved in my grandchildren's lives and since I couldn't do sports with them, I wanted to introduce them to the arts. It was a nice way to be involved with them one on one, teaching them to paint. My grandson, Ryan, made many pieces with charcoals and I surprised him by having the one I liked best professionally framed and now it hangs in his mother's living room. I tried to interest them in poetry and Alex writes when he gets an assignment in school and gets top grades. He also likes my poems very much. I never thought I could write a book and now I am now showing them that I can. I ask them who taught them how to cook and they say I did. I taught the boys how to cook and be gentlemen. Now I am not taking all the credit here. They have a mother and father that work. Carol Lee has her own business and we know how much time that takes with five children.

From generation to generation, though, no matter how busy we were with our work and our lives, we always have been a family of gardeners. Carol Lee and Peppy keep a vegetable garden, as I did, my mother did, and my grandaddy did. They also keep house, shop for food, cook, buy their clothes, and do their laundry. They go to their sports events and help with homework. The boys became Eagle Scouts, so someone is doing something right. They have a big yard so their friends can come over, a tree house that they can sleep in, a basketball court, and a trampoline. They know how to hunt and fish like their great grandaddy, though it was their father who taught them. They all have their game licenses. Of course, I could go on and on but can't forget they all go to church every Sunday, too. Patrick, my oldest grandson, volunteers at the Double H Ranch, the Hole in the Woods camp that Paul Newman and Charley Wood started in the Adirondacks years ago for very ill children.

*Amy*

Amy was our first grandchild, born a year after Carol Lee and Peppy were married. I remember the hospital waiting room was filled with people the night Carol Lee gave birth. It was March 15, 1984—the Ides of March—a little after 11 o'clock. Barbara Mandrell was performing at the Glens Falls Civic Center a few blocks away. All the families were at the hospital, too many people to count, for Peppy has a lot of brothers and sisters. On my daughter's side, it was just Nick and myself. I don't remember if there were enough seats for us all. We waited for hours. Finally the doctor came in and said that, "We have to do a C-section." I remember asking, "How long before we see the baby?" He said, "Five minutes." I said, "Go for it!" I was so excited I didn't even think to ask her husband.

I was so happy that I was going to see my first grandchild in five minutes after waiting nine long months that I just couldn't wait any longer. Next thing I knew, there she was, a little girl. I will never forget what her grandpa said as he bent over and looked at her: "Most babies aren't beautiful when they are born, but Carol Lee's and Peppy's baby is the most beautiful baby in the world." We didn't get to hold her until the next day, though.

Before the baby came home from the hospital, her Mom and Dad were picking out some baby names that I didn't like. I told my husband and he yelled out at me very loudly, "Let them pick out whatever name they want." That is when I told him that the name they wanted was Elijah. Well, Nick changed his tune and said, "I have to talk to them about this right away." He drove to the hospital and said to them, "How can you give this beautiful baby a name like that? A name you can't pronounce! Are you really going to make this child go through life with a name like Elijah?" I was glad Grandpa put his two cents in. The next day we went to the hospital and Peppy said, "How do you like the name Amy?" That's when Grandpa and I did a little soft shoe and sang "Once in Love with Amy."

Carol Lee got so many flowers and baby gifts of toys, clothes, and blankets that it took two truckloads to get it all home. She felt bad for the young girl next to her in the maternity ward who didn't receive anything at all so Carol Lee kept offering her flowers.

For the first 10 years of Amy's life she was at my house more than she was at home. I was much younger then, so we played house a lot. I had a whole floor fixed up for her with a toy grocery store, kitchen, and nursery. She had music and books and she had a whole wardrobe at my house. I got up every morning to take her to school and on our way to school we discussed the weather and what was happening on the lake. After we passed the lake we said our prayers until we reached the school, asking God to help us be like Him today. Every night I read Bible stories to her and we listened to children's Bible stories on tape. Later when she learned to read, she would read *me* Bible stories. We loved to cuddle together and slept in the same king-size bed.

I asked Amy what she learned from her grandmother all these years and she told me nursery rhymes, Bible stories, songs ("Once in Love with Amy" and "Bicycle Built for Two"), organizational skills, housecleaning, taking care of flowers, making a bed with hospital corners, fashion and modeling, manners, grammar, and cooking. She remembered that praying and going to church was something we enjoyed doing together. She also learned "I can do anything I set my mind to" and "Never say 'I can't'" from me. She said, "I learned so many things from Grandma, too many to count. She took me on trips and introduced me to the world of painting as well as the beauty of photography. I love her for everything she has done for me."

In high school Amy was a good student and was very talented at art and photography like me. In her senior year, she won Best in Show for her photography. I offered her $500 for her winning picture, but instead it hangs in her mother's house. She also earned honorable mention for her artwork and was written up in the newspaper. After high school, she went to Hudson Valley College for a year. Against our advice, she left school and came to work at the restaurant for a year, where she did a terrific job. Next she worked in a coffee shop, then went to work in her mother's store and soon after she became pregnant and had a beautiful baby boy named Enzo. He is the light of everybody's life. Enzo's dad, Seth, is a good father and Amy is a wonderful mother. She gives him all her attention and teaches him how to be a good boy. I really never have seen a mother be so good to her child as Amy is to Enzo. He is very smart, but don't all grandparents say that about their grandchildren? He really is intelligent, though. Now Amy wants to open her own business just like all the generations before her, so she is back in college taking business courses.

*Patrick*

Patrick is my second grandchild. It was so great having a boy. He was 10 ½ pounds when he was born. Looking through the nursery everyone was saying how beautiful he was and how he looked like my husband. I could not say that he was beautiful and couldn't see how anyone else could because he looked like a sumo wrestler to me. I called him Sumo a lot until Carol Lee said, "Mom, please

## My Life As I Lived It

don't call him that." I was afraid he was going to look like that when he grew up but he turned out to be the best looking kid I ever saw, so handsome he could be a model. He would look good even if he was dressed in rags.

When he was young I read Bible stories to him and Amy and when I asked them questions about the stories, he always raised his hand first, saying "I know! I know! I know!" and always wanting to answer the question whether he knew the answer or not. He just liked raising his hand first. He used to come over to my house and play house with Amy and my godchild, Felicia. One day when Patrick was three and Felicia was four, the kids were playing house and Patrick was going to "marry" Felicia. Well, they were "married" for about two years until one day Patrick tugged on my sleeve and very seriously said, "Grandma, please can I not be married to Felicia anymore?" I had to laugh.

Patrick's father taught all the boys how to hunt and fish at a camp they have in the Adirondacks. Patrick loves to go hunting with his father. He played freshman football at Lake George High School and he was so good we didn't want to miss a game. When he was running with the ball, it was so exciting I ran up and down the sidelines following him. He was the best player in his senior class. People came to see him play because of the thrill of watching him. He made All-County and All-State in high school and graduated from Lake George with a full scholarship to play football at Gunnery Prep School, then a four-year scholarship to college. He had several injuries, though. He broke his leg and had a steel rod put in it and he also tore his rotator cuff. He gave up football due to the injuries and pursued other interests like sailing. My husband was very upset that he gave up football, as my husband was a great football player and coach for most of his life. Patrick graduated from Salve Regina University in Newport, Rhode Island in 2010 with a degree in biology. He has always been considerate of his Grandma and Grandpa.

When I asked Patrick what he learned from me, he said, "Grandma taught me "Never say I can't." She also taught me an appreciation for painting and how to mix colors. She read me Bible stories when I was young and taught me how to be a good Christian. She taught me how to garden and take care of flowers, and how to cook chicken, turkey soup, lobster, and crab. She taught me the importance of hard work, too. I mowed the lawn for her and helped her whenever I could. She always liked when I spent time with her. I could feel her love for me. I appreciate everything Grandma has done for me and that was a lot!"

*Ryan*

Ryan, the third grandchild, was a hard delivery. Carol Lee wanted to have a natural childbirth. I do not know why the doctor agreed with her as he delivered the first two by Caesarian. I was there waiting for the birth when she hemorrhaged and they rushed her into delivery. The nurse told me she could die and the baby could die, too. The nurses were all crying and I was in shock. Nick was catering a home barbeque for someone and I called him and told him to come to the hospital right away. I warned him they might not be alive when he got here. When he finally arrived at the hospital it was all over, they told me mother and baby were fine. I could not grasp it even when I saw them. I still thought they were going to die. I never called and told my dear friends that I had my third grandchild until six months later because it took me that long to get over the trauma. I remember Ryan being a very good grandchild growing up and was no trouble at all. He has always been considerate, helping me with groceries and mowing our lawn.

He attended Rose-Hulman Institute of Technology in Indiana. He is very smart and is studying chemical engineering. He told me he had to take English and he was having a hard time of it. I encouraged him to enjoy writing and look at what I have done with it. The next semester I talked to him and he said he was doing better and not having such a hard time. I said, "See I told you that you could do it. You may become a writer some day just like your grandma." He said he wasn't going to make a career out of writing. I told him that he might develop a cure for some disease and want to write about it someday. Now he's attending college in Buffalo.

Ryan and I have a lot we enjoy together. He is also very handsome. No girls in his life so far, as he always made his education the most important priority. He became an Eagle Scout, as did his brother Patrick. During his high school days he played football for a while and then gave it up. All the boys loved to hunt up at their camp. One day Ryan shot a four-point deer and everybody was shocked, including him. Some men hunt their whole lives and never kill a deer, never mind a four-pointer.

He loves to travel and I hope to travel with him someday. One Christmas Nick and I took Ryan, his brother Alex, his youngest sister, Emily, and their parents on a cruise for Christmas. I had been on cruises before and I wanted to watch them enjoy their first one. It was quite wonderful. Ryan and I talk on the phone and correspond by email. I just love to talk to him and Nick and I enjoy his company as much as he enjoys being with us.

We've taken Ryan fishing, lobstering, and crabbing. One of his favorite foods is lobster. He would even ask me to make it for him for breakfast. He told me, "I love hearing about my grandmother and grandfather's trips because I would like to be a world traveler someday. Grandma and I love playing cards. When I was young, she told me Bible stories and how to be a good Christian. She also taught me never to say 'I can't' because I can do anything I decide I want to do."

*Alex*

I babysat Alex once when he was young, maybe three or four years old. I had a bad back and I was lying on the floor to exercise it. Alex thought that I wanted to play horsey and he kept jumping on me. I kept saying, "No! No!" but then he came at me from the front, thinking that I wanted to play bullfighting. So he kept ramming his head into mine. I couldn't get up and begged him to stop doing it but he didn't stop because he thought we were having fun. The only one getting hurt was me, at first my back and then my head. I thought I had my chance to get up but he rammed me in the face again, giving me my first bloody nose of my life. I thought he broke it because there was so much blood everywhere. Needless to say that was the last time I babysat that grandchild. Alex has been wonderful to me ever since. My friends tell me how very well liked he is. He is sincerely interested in others' lives and is the perfect gentleman. He opens and closes the car door for me. He really is wonderful to everybody. He always comes to visit me, gives me a kiss, and asks me if there is anything he can do for me. When I call him to help me with the computer, which is often, he comes over right away.

Alex told me, "Grandma taught me the things my brothers and sisters also learned, such as enjoying our religion and having good morals. She taught me how to cook and she gave me a piano so I could take piano lessons. Now I'm very busy with football, baseball, basketball, and other sports. I'm also working on my Eagle Scout project, so I don't have time right now for the piano. I hope to take it up again one day, as Grandma tells me it's good for de-stressing."

Alex played quarterback and running back for his football team, for which and he also punts and kicks. He's an excellent player and makes headlines in the local newspaper every week, like "Labruzzo does it all." One week he scored the winning touchdown. Another week he scored four touchdowns to win the game.

It seems like he's always winning the game for Lake George. He is an all-around talented athlete and he is very good looking like the rest of the boys. They could all be models if you ask me. Alex has blue eyes and light hair where the rest of the family has dark hair and brown eyes. Alex never sees me without kissing me. He loves his grandmother, I can tell and his grandmother loves him, he can tell.

*Emily*

I wrote this letter while Carol Lee was pregnant with Emily, a letter I pictured Emily writing to me where she would say:

Hi Grandma,

Mom told me I am one year old today. Thirteen years before I was born you named me Emily. That was when Patrick was born instead of me. Only you and I know you picked that name for me. Mom and Dad thought they picked it because you didn't say anything. I know how happy you were when they said. "What do you think of Emily?" You quietly said, "That's nice." You never said, "That's the name I wanted!" because you were afraid they would change it.

See, Grandma I know everything! I am sorry you waited so long for me, but here I am making everyone happy. Mom and Dad love me so much. I have the most special parents in the whole world. That is why I am always smiling.

My big sister, Amy, was 16 when I was born. She has been like a second Mom to me. She is always going to be there for me. My big brother, Patrick, was 14. He is so gentle and loving to me, just like my Dad. Ryan was 9 and Alex was 6. They make me laugh so much, making funny faces and jumping all around. Before I was born, everyone wanted me to be a girl. Remember when you gave Mom a coffee cup that said, "It's a girl" and you made her drink from it everyday while I was in her tummy? When Mom went for her ultrasound, you were dressed up in pink, carrying a pink doll. You told all the nurses and doctors to "Think Pink." When you had the baby shower for me, you bought me 12 pink outfits. You sure did have fun buying them. The cake your friend Pam made was really beautiful, with a baby lying on her tummy on a pink blanket and wearing a pink diaper. Grandma, I saw everything, and so did God. God said to me, "Emily, you go into this loving family, be a good girl and make them all happy." Yes, God. I will do just that.

Love,
Emily

One Christmas I bought the kids shares of McDonald's stock so I could teach them about the stock market. I had the boys watch Jim Cramer's show, "Mad Money," with me on television. He is a wild man about stocks and fun to watch and we learned at the same time. Emily, then eight years old, was the happiest about her stock because she thought she could go to McDonald's any time and eat for free. Ryan and Alex had to explain to her how it really works.

Emily likes to tell stories and a lot of her stories are quite convincing. When she tells me a story I believe her and then I think to ask, "Fiction or non-fiction?" Eventually I figured out that most of her stories are fiction. I hope she becomes a writer when she gets older because she has all the talent for writing fiction. Emily was on the cover of an *I Love NY* magazine and I hope to see her one day on the cover of many of her own fiction books.

Emily is now a typical, beautiful teenaged girl. Her favorite sport is volleyball. I used to love playing volleyball, too. I can't believe she gets herself up a 4:30 in the morning to get ready for school. I think she spends most of that time straightening her hair. Nobody wants to have curly hair today. I think her curly hair was prettier, but maybe I am out of date.

I'm teaching Emily everything I taught the other children, and now that she's a teenager, I'm trying to teach her good morals and how to be a good person, so she can be as good as she is beautiful.

### *Christmas Keys*

*'Twas the night before Christmas*
*Down in the Keys Grandma and Grandpa*
*Were waiting to see*

*Amy, Patrick,*
*Alex, and Ryan*
*If they don't get here soon*
*We'll be crying*

*Pop-Pops and I wait*
*Day and night*
*For all the grandkids*
*To come into sight*

*Maybe they're with Santa*
*In his sleigh*
*And it's his gift to us*
*That they're on their way*

*So we'll hang up our stockings*
*And go to bed*
*We'll rest our eyes*
*And cover our heads*

*Then tomorrow morning*
*In the Florida Keys*
*Not a sound will be heard*
*Not even a breeze*

*We'll get out of bed*
*And open our eyes*
*Yes, Santa was here*
*He left us a surprise*

*And guess what we found*
*Hidden under our tree*
*It was Alex, Ryan,*
*Patrick and Amy*

*Then we heard Santa exclaim*
*From over the seas*
*Merry Christmas, Grandma and Grandpa*
*In the Florida Keys*

(From *Easy-Reading Poetry* by Caroline Lee Cutro)

# We are retired now

This is it. I can't take it anymore. I sent my husband to the store with a note to buy three things: eggs, milk, and orange juice. Not just any kind of orange juice but Tropicana, the only kind I drink. He's brought home other brands of orange juice before and I've had to bring them back to the store and get Tropicana. I've made a big issue about this before, but I stressed it again and wrote it on the grocery list I gave him: "Tropicana with lots of pulp." I went over it with him before he left and said one more time, "Nick, it must say *lots of pulp*, it's written across the top of the container." "Lots of pulp" was also written on the grocery list, which contained only three items, so what could go wrong?

Well, he met a few friends, went shopping, and by the time he came home (sometime after 11:30 o'clock) I was sleeping. I woke up at around 2 in the morning, and being thirsty I went to the refrigerator and was glad to see that he had bought the groceries, including my favorite juice, Tropicana. I reached for the container and then I saw it. In disbelief, I read the label a couple of times: "No pulp."

No pulp. No pulp? With a big sigh I said to myself, "This can't be. I can't take this anymore. Where did I go wrong? What didn't I say? How didn't it say it? What could I have written differently? How could this happen? That's it, I just can't take it!" I thought, "In a few days I will have been married for 39 years. I don't know how I made it this far and I sure don't know how I'll make it to 40 years." I remember when we had a big party for our 25th anniversary, I thought, "My God, I didn't think I'd make it." I remember thinking that the next 25 years should be easier.

Well, wrong! Now 39 years is upon me and how do I make it to 40? I must come up with some idea. I must save myself because I'm really desperate. Then, at 2 in the morning, a wonderful idea came to me. I'll write a book to save myself from frustration, stress, anxiety, impatience, aggravation, anger, hurt and all the other adjectives that apply, in addition to simply losing my mind. That's it, I thought. So I lay back down to sleep thinking that writing a book would be my salvation. I'll write it in the morning, I thought, but no, that won't work. I must save myself now because tomorrow might be too late. So with pad and pen in hand this book was born and so was a new life for me. Instead of experiencing those negative emotions, the next time feelings like that come over me, I'll say "Great, more material for my book! I'm saved!"

So I put the pen down and went back to bed expecting to sleep with a contented smile on my face. How pleasantly I drifted off to peaceful sleep, knowing I would have another story to tell tomorrow. I couldn't wait to see what the next day would bring. Now instead of hating all these irritations, they would find a welcome home in my book. Would it happen that way? I will just have to wait and see.

The next morning, I read the first pages of my book to my husband, to see what kind of response I would get for the rest of the day. Believe it or not, that day went well. Maybe he was watching himself. Now I'm not saying he was perfect by any means. In reality I probably just wasn't looking hard enough. Nothing bad happened, however, so there were no stories that day for my book.

The next day was Sunday. By 1:30 in the afternoon, I felt like I had gone through 24 hours already. It was like taking care of a kid whose plans went wrong and like any good mother, I tried to help to make everything come out right. My kids are all adults now but I still have one big kid to take care of—Nick.

Nick had plans to go to the Miami Dolphins football game with his friends. Even though the stadium is two hours from our house in the Keys, as men are so unorganized, no exact time was set for when these friends were to pick up my husband to go to the game. So Nick and I went to church and out for breakfast and when we arrived home, there was a message from his friend Bobby on the answering machine: "Where are you? We're leaving now. If you get home on time call my wife Susan. She's coming up and she can drop you off at the bar."

"What bar?" Nick asked. He called Susan and she didn't know. She said Bobby told her that Nick would know because he'd been there before. Nick told me he'd been there once two years ago and didn't remember any details. He said he wasn't going unless he made contact with his friends first. I could already tell this was really going to ruin my day. He would sit in front of the television for 10 hours watching football and I'd have to listen to it as I do every week, all afternoon and evening on Sunday, as well as on Monday night and sometimes Thursday night. I had planned to enjoy the quietness of my home alone, but now my day would be ruined. I knew that Nick's day would also be ruined because he'd missed going to the game and we would likely not get along all day.

I decided that I must get into action fast, thus several phone calls were made. Unfortunately nobody answered, but we left messages everywhere. I said to Nick encouragingly, "It will be okay, you go, I'll get in touch with your friends by phone somehow. At least you can go to some bar close to the stadium and watch the first game on television and then take a taxi and meet them at the usual spot in the parking lot of the stadium." So he left with Susan as I happily stayed home alone manning the phones.

Now I knew all of this could have been avoided if we had come home right after church, but Nick said "Let's go to breakfast." Well, to his surprise he cut it too close and the group left without him.

You know how nice it would have been if he said, "Dear, we have to hurry home after church so I can help you with a few things before I leave for the game?" But he didn't say that. Never, never, never in my married life has he ever said something like that, but a girl can dream, can't she? For all these years I've been having these fantasies of the way married life should be. It was always so perfect in the movies in the 1940s and 1950s, where everyone got married and lived happily ever after. I never saw a movie in which they married and the husband watched sports on television for the rest of his life.

The phone rang and it was his friend who gave me the directions for where Nick was supposed to go. Great, I'll call him on his cell phone and at least now I could enjoy the rest of my day.

Still having that old movie fantasy, I waited until two in the morning for him to come home, feeling like I wanted to be hugged and then drift off to sleep together. When he came home, he jumped into bed because he was very tired from the long day. So I went to get into bed with him but his dog, Tennessee, got there first. He immediately started petting her and they were both contented, but not me. I couldn't take it so I went into the other bedroom and did the next best thing: I hugged my big pillow, which was perfect for such occasions, and went to sleep.

The next night I got in bed first, ready to hug Nick and fall asleep in his arms but the dog's timing was once again better than mine. I'm so glad that I have another bedroom and a big pillow to comfort me. I don't know how many other women have a husband that loves his dog like Nick loves Tennessee. That dog gets all the attention and love and Nick has nothing left over for me. It is sickening to hear him say things like "Come to daddy," "Daddy's girl," "Come here, baby," "Look how she loves to have her ears rubbed," or "Look, hon, you have to see this." He even leaves the TV on for her and makes sure she's comfortable if he has to leave

## My Life As I Lived It

her at home, which is rare because she usually goes wherever he goes. He goes grocery shopping often for me, but I think he only does it so he can buy her treats. I believe he has never gone into a store without buying her something. Being such a thoughtful man, you'd think he's brought me flowers. Guess how many times that happened in 39 years—twice!

Do you know what my daughter, a loving mother with a lot of insight, told me? She said, "Seeing how you complain so much of lacking Dad's attention, maybe it would have been best if you were born a dog." I think I'll let my husband read this hoping some positive changes may take place without me having to say, "Woof, woof."

From bad to worse, you won't believe where he went tonight. He went to pick up my daughter's dog, Ivory, a Bichon Frise. My daughter was going on a two-week vacation and guess who is the best one to take care of her dog? No one better than Nick, of course. My daughter's dog is also a bed jumper so I guess I know where I'll spend the next two weeks and it won't be in a bed with two dogs and their caretaker.

They just arrived home and I have retreated to my other bedroom where my big pillow is waiting. I think my pillow will be Burt Reynolds tonight. "Coming Burt," I say and I pretend Burt says "Goodnight, Caroline, honey." Sometimes instead of Burt Reynolds it's Brad Pitt. I can pretend it's someone different every night. Aren't I lucky?

The first day of the two-week vacation—my daughter's, certainly not mine—my girlfriend, Carol, called me before she took off for a Christmas cruise. She heard yelling in the background during our conversation and said, "Whose kids are there with you?" I said, "Two dogs." Nick was yelling "Stop it, quiet down, what's the matter with them?" I asked myself, "What's the matter with *you*?" He expected them to listen to him. I told him to let them go, maybe they'll tire themselves out and we'll have quiet for the rest of the day.

The last time Ivory was here we put the dogs' water bowls in the kitchen but those dogs made a mess and Nick isn't one to leave his shoes at the door, so needless to say I had a muddy kitchen floor. This time I decided to put their drinking water on our enclosed porch on our grass rug. One morning I noticed a big wet spot on my grass rug on the porch, but far from the dogs' drinking water. I touched the wet spot and then I called Nick and said "Look, this spot is wet but their drinking water is way over there." Nick answered nonchalantly, "She must have peed" as if it was okay. As I cleaned up the pee, I thought that I'd like to put Cindy's dog to sleep and Nick, too. I have a girlfriend, Leta, who always tells her dog to behave or she'll put her to sleep. You know I might just try that someday and see how it works out. Anyway I told Nick that he had better take the dogs out before he takes a shower, making sure to walk Ivory first thing. I said that I'd keep the porch door closed in the morning so Ivory didn't think she could do her business in there.

I guess I could have let my house be trashed for the next two weeks and blamed the dogs like my friends blame their kids but that's not me. I'm a clean freak. You'd think I wouldn't even have a dog. Yes, that was a mistake, and a bigger mistake every time I had to clean up one of *their* mistakes. Nick took the dogs out without leashes, even though we live in a retirement development now that has a leash law. Of course, the dogs took off and greeted all the ladies who were out walking, completely ignoring Nick's calls. Nothing like being the conversation of the day in the neighborhood! He will be written up in the next neighborhood newsletter for sure.

Nick's dog has to have her own shelf in my food closet for all her treats. Tennessee weighs only 13 pounds, so she shouldn't need much room in the closet, but if that closet was empty, Nick would have all the shelves filled for her. Although his dog's name is

Tennessee, Nick calls her "Tenny Honey." Every time I hear it I get sick. The dog is "Honey" and I am just "Hon." I've been married for nearly 40 years and I'm still just "Hon." "Hon" just doesn't have any emotion behind it like "Honey" has. You know what I mean.

We had another Bichon Frise before Tennessee that was named Bijou. She was a great dog. She loved Nick *and* me. The vet said it would be good to breed her one time, so we did. She delivered four beautiful puppies and Bijou was a wonderful mother. We kept the puppies in the kitchen because Bijou didn't want to be around those nuts all the time, although she was always there for their feedings. I kept the puppies for quite a while and had a lot of fun with them but they were a lot of work.

We had Bijou for 14 wonderful years. For better or worse, richer or poorer, in sickness and in health, until death do us part. When she got very sick we went to a shrine at St. Joseph Cathedral in Montreal where Nick and I prayed for Bijou's recovery. At the shrine there are 300 steps that people climbed in hopes of a miracle. Nick and I spent the day there climbing the steps and then on our knees praying in church. We even left a bit of her fur there. Unfortunately, things only got worse so I talked with my priest in the Keys about it and he told me that I was lucky to be able to put the dog to sleep to relieve her of her pain and misery. Everybody at church was praying for me to have the strength to do it. We had a ceremony of good-byes then my veterinarian and his assistant came to the house and let me hold Bijou in my arms while they told me how it would be quick and that she wouldn't feel a thing. It only took about a minute. Afterwards we had her cremated and put her ashes in an urn. I took the urn in bed with me and laid her next to my stomach. When I went for a car ride, I took her, too. After a while I sat her on my nightstand.

Nick and I made a deal that the first one who dies gets to take Bijou's ashes with them in their coffin. I think Bijou loved me more than Nick but a deal is a deal. Now that Tennessee is in the picture, I think it's time for a new deal where I get Bijou. I told Nick that since Tennessee loves him more, he gets her in his coffin. I said, "If you die before her, I'll have her put to sleep so she can be with you." He said "That's awful, that's terrible. How could you do that, don't you care?" He didn't like that I would purposely put her to sleep to be with him. I said that I didn't see the problem. "I think you would look nice in your coffin holding treats in your hand for your Tenny Honey." So goes another day.

When my daughter's dog, Ivory, squatted in the living room, I was at the end of my rope. What led to this? Well, I made a big dinner with a roast and all the trimmings, which I do not intend to do again while two dogs are living in my house. I was trying to navigate the kitchen to serve the meal I lovingly prepared while Nick was preparing the dogs' (or maybe I should say "the girls'") dinner. He was moving all over the kitchen, getting in my way, like a brick wall with, of course, no sense. How come men can't see what you're doing? They're so into themselves that you bump them, push them, do a little shove, and nothing. You expect them to say "Am I in your way? Sorry, Hon." (Certainly not "Honey" because that's reserved for Tennessee.)

Instead he was deeply engrossed in preparing the dogs' dinner. I couldn't take it anymore so I said, "Don't you think your timing is bad?" We all ate together—Nick, his girls, and me. If he could have, he probably would have put napkins around their necks and let them sit with us at the dinner table, too. He sensed that "Tenny Honey" had to go, so he took her outside. He usually took the two dogs out together but this time he didn't and I wondered why didn't he take Ivory, too.

When he came in, Ivory ran for the door. I said, "Nick, she's got to go," but it was too late. She didn't have to run to the door twice, she didn't even have to run to the grass rug on the porch. She just peed right there on my living room rug. I guess she was making sure Nick wouldn't leave her behind next time. Surely Nick would stop what he was doing and clean up the pee. After all, having two dogs in the house was not my idea. I waited and waited and finally I said, "What are we going to do?" He said, "Clean it up." To be clear, he didn't mean *he'd* clean it up, he was telling *me* to clean it up. I wanted to say no and wait for him to do it, but I'd wait and wait but it would never happen. He'd win, so I figured I may as well do it right away, but before cleaning it up I'd like to stick Nick's nose in it. Another fantasy, I guess.

That same night there was a thunderstorm in the middle of the night and Tenny woke Nick up so he thought she had to go. So he got up and let her out the door without a leash and she took off because she was scared of the thunderstorm. Nick called her to come back, but she wouldn't come. He went after her in his underwear, running barefoot down the middle of street screaming, "Tenny! Tenny! Tenny!" It took about half hour to finally get her and I had a big laugh when they came through the door, both of them soaking wet. I was having a good laugh at what the neighbors would be talking about the next day.

If I could rewrite the end of this evening it would read: They sat holding hands and looking into each others eyes, as the candlelight sparkled on their champagne glasses. Even after years of marriage, the romance was still there. (This is definitely a fantasy.)

# A Caribbean cruise and my game show debut

We went on a Caribbean cruise for our 50th wedding anniversary on the Oasis of the Sea, which was the largest of the cruise liners at the time. Even at 220,000 tons and 16 decks high, it was not like being on a ship at all. It had a two-story mall that extended the whole length and width of the ship and you could look up to the sky from the middle of the mall. There were cables running overhead from one side of the ship to the other, where daredevils could whiz across the distance of over 80 feet. There were also two rock climbing walls for the thrill seekers, but I was happy just to watch all the action. The ship's best feature for me was that it didn't feel like it was moving at all. It took the waves and you could not feel them. I like my cruises to be calm, as I have been on too many rough seas in my lifetime. There were big Vegas-style shows, several theaters, many places to eat, bars and discos, Central Park for walking around, a carousel, an ice skating rink, and 20 pools. There were ice cream stands, which I did indulge in and one day I had my first corn dog. They had pizza and all kinds of stuff to eat around the pool, but I only spent one day up on that deck. No sitting in the sun for me, I did enough of that my whole young life.

Then there was a surf simulator, which had even little kids surfing along with the hotshot surfers. I just sat and watched them and thought if I was younger, nothing would stop me from surfing on that ship! There was also a 9-hole golf course for adults and a smaller one for kids. There was so much to see and do that Nick and I decided we'd have to take another trip to see it all. We just can't wait to do it again.

Many mornings we'd spend in the room. I'd order room service for breakfast and lunch because that kept Nick in the room writing the book I have been trying to get him to write for 30 years. I am so proud of him for getting so much done, writing for hours at a time. If we left our room for breakfast we didn't get back to writing because there were too many distractions. We had a beautiful room with a patio and wall-to-wall sliding glass doors that gave us a wonderful view of the ocean, perfect for writing. The cruise stopped in Nassau, St. Maarten, and St. Thomas, but Nick and I had seen the islands before so we didn't go ashore. Our daughters and their husbands, who surprised us by joining us on the trip for our anniversary, got off the ship at the stops. It was wonderful having Cindy, Crockett, Carol Lee, and Peppy on the ship with us. We'd all go to dinner and a show every night. Most nights we would eat late (for me anyway) at around 9 o'clock then they would all go to the casino and I'd go too bed, too full from that late dinner to go out or even to go to sleep with such a full stomach. Carol Lee or Peppy always took me to my room to make sure I was okay, which I appreciated so much. I am used to eating no later than 5 o'clock.

One night I heard there was going to be a show called Love and Marriage, which was supposed to be like "The Newlywed Game." I told the kids I wanted to be on stage and believe me, I made sure I was picked. I sat in the front row and when they asked who was married the longest I jumped up and down, even with my bad knees. People applauded and I bowed and they called me up on the stage, of course. Nick didn't seem as thrilled to be chosen, however. They picked two more couples, one just married, the other married for a while, and, of course, we were married the longest. Peppy called Cindy and Crockett's room to tell them I got on the show. They didn't think I would get picked with 1,380 people to choose from. Well, what fun that show was. I had the crowd laughing at every answer I gave. I didn't want to win, I just wanted to enjoy myself and have the crowd laugh a lot and they sure did. I became the best-known celebrity on board the ship! Everywhere I went people stopped me to say they either were at the show or saw me on the TV in their room. One lady said she didn't feel good that night because she had a headache and went to her room to lie down. She watched the show on TV and laughed so much that after the show was over she felt wonderful. She thanked me very much and told me I was just great.

I was loving all the attention. It was just what movie stars must feel like. The people stopped me in the casinos, on deck, in the elevator, standing in line for dinner, coming out of dinner, even while I sat and ate dinner. My life of stardom was just a couple of days, but what a wonderful feeling. I will never forget being on that stage in front of a 1,380 people and knowing that the other 4,000 on the ship watched me on the TV in their room. They replayed the show three times a day on TV. Even the waiters and workers on the ship saw the show on TV and told me how funny they thought it was. One guy stopped me and said, "I saw you on the telly." He must have been British. It was really nice that my kids saw and enjoyed all the attention their old mother was getting. I have a DVD they gave me of the show, which will be fun to show the grandkids back at home.

# The horse farm

Nick and I made it through 52 years of marriage because we spent most of those years buying and running businesses and houses together. One of the least successful ventures was the Thoroughbred farm we started. I wasn't crazy about the idea, but we agreed to buy a small barn and have just three horses. Even though we had an agreement, however, Nick did not keep his end of the bargain. At one time we had 42 horses and 13 stables at the Saratoga racetrack in New York. We raced our horses all over the country. While I don't much like talking about those horses, I will say the fun part was on opening day of the season at Saratoga. We would have a brunch out at our farm, which we called Boardwalk Farm after our restaurant, which is where we earned all the money we ended up throwing away on those horses!

All the cooking for the brunch took place at the restaurant and the employees brought the food to the farm, along with tables and chairs for the party. Our employees loved working that brunch. A lot of friends would come, maybe 50 or so, the men all dressed to kill with their sharp suits and the women with their dresses and hats.

When we bought the rundown 90-acre farm, it had a barn that should have been torn down but Nick decided he wanted to renovate the whole thing instead. Then he gave it to me to decorate, but told me to remember it was a barn, which only made me want to make it look like the Taj Mahal. I put mirrored verticals on the windows that looked out over the farm and a little back porch. Inside were gray walls and carpet and a gray velvet couch and chair. The cabinets I designed were gray, as was the refrigerator, stove, and sink. Behind the corner sink I had designed strips of curved glass mirror to match the verticals on the windows. I know it sounds all gray but my accents were done in mirror and chrome. The mirror behind the couch was very striking, while the table and chairs were chrome with seats in gray velvet to match the couch. There was a gray tablecloth and chrome candles, and gray napkins with chrome rings around them. The end tables were glass-topped chrome with two different chrome lamps. Across from the couch were two seven-foot tall chrome stands with a chrome and glass table between them on which sat a nearly one-of-a-kind gray TV.

The rest of the apartment—a bedroom, an office, and a bathroom—were similarly decorated. It was so interesting to see the people at the brunch come up to see our apartment. I had to go in the apartment first so I could see the looks on their faces and hear the gasps. They could not believe their eyes. They thought they were in a Fifth Avenue penthouse apartment, which was just what I was going for. Every year when people came to the brunch they had to go up to see the apartment again. I would tell them that Nick had said to remember I was decorating a barn, which is exactly what I did in the second apartment where the manager lived.

There were cameras on the horses' birthing stable so we could watch from the comfort of our apartment. One night we knew there was going to be a birth and my granddaughter Amy was there playing a music box with a bride and groom dancing on top. When it was time for the delivery, we all went down to watch. It was like a miracle. That filly was born kicking! It's hard to believe they're so strong at birth, but I remember being black and blue after I delivered one myself. You must get them standing as soon as possible, then you know they will be okay. Since Amy was there with us, I asked her what she wanted to name the filly. She said, "Dancing and Love." She got the name from the music box upstairs, which I thought was sweet.

We sold a Thoroughbred horse named Dusty Darling to a horse trainer who trained him to be a trick horse that appeared on the soap opera, "Another World" and in commercials. Dusty Darling didn't make it big time with us, but he did make it big time in front of the cameras. The trainer could do incredible stunts with that horse. He told us he could even make the horse poop inside a garbage pail!

# My cabin after 50 years

My mother left me our family cabin. It's really a cottage but we call it a cabin because the others nearby are log cabins. One summer we renovated it to make it the same as it was when my mother and I had it 50 years earlier. We kept it green and white on the outside but otherwise had to nearly gut it. My grandchildren helped with a lot of the work because they were off from school and we could not hire help because everyone is busy working during the summer in the Adirondacks.

During the renovation of the cabin I could not walk as I had torn meniscus in both knees, and I had to be lifted out of my chair where I sat all day giving directions. My grandchildren had never painted before and while they did the best they could, it drove me crazy. At the time I was very frustrated but everything turned out okay. We had Nick's friend put in a ceiling in one of the rooms and I had a girlfriend put up wallpaper. We also hired someone to put on a new roof and install a new septic system. Before we could begin the work, though, everything had to be ripped out of the house. So my 18-year-old grandson Patrick and his buddy took about 10 truckloads of stuff out the cabin. Rugs, flooring, kitchen appliances—what a mess. We would all leave Lake George at about eight o'clock in the morning and return at four in the afternoon, day after day, all summer long. My grandson Ryan, who was 15 at the time, put concrete blocks under the building to strengthen the floor in the kitchen and living room. Nick did too many things to mention while I inspected everyone's work like a foreman.

A day or two during the week I went to Lowe's and rode around in a motorized cart picking out carpeting for the living room and bedroom floors, as well as kitchen and bathroom flooring. Next I got new appliances and kitchen cabinets, along with lighting and bedding and much more. When all the work was finished, it was time for me to decorate, which was not hard because I had a lot of experience and it was a joy for me. I painted the inside of the house the same colors they had been at the beginning and also kept the other details of the original cottage. There was one thing that would be different from the old days, however—I wanted it to focus on the past seven generations.

Right when you walk in the door, the walls tell a story. On the first wall there is a large oil painting of my grandaddy's one-room log cabin, which is where it all started. Alongside that painting there are three antique photographs, one of my great grandmother and great grandfather on their wedding day, one of them on their 25th wedding anniversary, and one of my grandaddy, their son. There is a picture of Grandaddy and his wife Carrie's wedding announcement and wedding photograph. Then there's a photo of Carrie and her two young daughters, Caroline and Ethel. Their mother died soon after that picture was taken. There's a photo of my mother and father's wedding and on another wall, there's one of my father and his mother and father on the Lee side. On another wall there are pictures of the houses and stores and restaurants we owned, and in another room I have pictures of all seven generations of my family, including all the wedding pictures.

Looking at the photos of all those generations of my family, it's amazing to realize that I have lived through 13 presidents so far, from the time I was born in 1938 and Franklin Delano Roosevelt was president. My grandaddy, who lived from 1891 to 1964, saw 14 presidents in office, starting with Benjamin Harrison. My great grandfather, who lived from 1866 to 1935, also lived through

14 presidents, starting with Andrew Johnson. While the first 16 presidents—from George Washington through Abraham Lincoln—were in office while my ancestors were still in Germany, in total, my family has lived through 27 presidents since coming to the United States.

I call this home my cottage of memories. In one bedroom there is my mother and father's bedroom set where my brother and I were conceived. I hung 8 x 10-inch baby pictures of my brother and me in beautiful white birch frames that were handmade by an artist, Bobby Foote, who dated my cousin, Dorothy, when we were young. In the living room is the antique sewing machine that I learned to sew on. There is also an oil painting of summer, winter, spring, and fall that I painted on one wall and a pastel I did on another. I could not hang my watercolors or pen-and-inks because there wasn't any wall space left, so I had them laminated and store them at the cabin.

In another bedroom, I put two pieces of furniture that belonged to my father's mother, including a cedar closet and cedar chest that I always admired. Also from my father's mother I have a Little Red Riding Hood ceramic teapot, sugar bowl, and milk pitcher, which sit together on the kitchen cabinet. There are many other collectibles from my grandparents in other rooms.

Now 50 years later the cabin is just mine, my little getaway in Minerva, New York, in the heart of the Adirondack Mountains. I never intend to sell the cottage. I have noted this in my will. The whole cottage tells a story, with all my family's antiques, photos, and treasures, along with this book and my book of poems. I always wanted to know more about my grandparents, and as I hung these pictures on the wall, I decided to write *My Life as I Lived It* so future generations of my family would know a little about their ancestors and all about me. For whomever is reading my book, I hope you will think about writing a memoir for *your* future generations.

### *By the Sea*

*I walk along the beach each day*
*Leaving my footprints along the way*
*Until a wave comes drifting by*
*Taking them with the tide.*

*There will be a day*
*When you won't see*
*My footprints*
*Down by the sea.*

(from *Easy-Reading Poetry* by Caroline Lee Cutro)

Made in the USA
Charleston, SC
26 April 2014